A Place to Call Home

The first 90 years of Hornsey Housing Trust

Rosie Boughton

©Rosie Boughton
Foreword ©June Barnes
Final Chapter ©Euan Barr

First published 2023

All rights reserved. No part of this publication may be reproduced, published or transmitted in any form or by any means, electronic, mechanical or otherwise, without the prior written permission of the Hornsey Housing Trust, the authors or their heirs.

Published by:
Hornsey Housing Trust
62 Mayfield Road
London N8
www.hornsey-ht.co.uk

Front cover: View down Ferme Park Road N8 towards Alexandra Palace.
©Hornsey Housing Trust

Design by Bob Cree
Printed by City Printing Limited, Hornsey Rd, N7
Photographs ©Tim Wilson unless otherwise stated

Disclaimer: The information given in this book is believed to be correct at the time of publication. No responsibility can be accepted by the authors or publisher for errors or omissions.

ISBN: 978-1-3999-7068-6

Contents

Foreword by June Barnes, Chair 4
Setting the scene 6
Early growth: 1933–1939 16
The war years: 1939–1945 32
The post-war decade: 1945–1955 42
Consolidation: 1955–1970 53
Modernisation: 1970–1985 64
Expansion: 1985–2000 76
Recent years: 2000–2023 86
Hornsey Housing Trust today, and looking ahead
by Euan Barr, Chief Executive 105
Acknowledgements 114
Bibliography and Archives 115
Contributors 118

Author's Note

This is 'a' history of Hornsey Housing Trust, not 'the' history. The sources we have are patchy: for example, the minutes of the Tenants' Assistance Fund Committee, which give such a rich flavour of the early years of the Trust, were only maintained until 1956; and we do not have many formal records of the period between 1985 and 2014. On the plus side, I have had access to an unpublished biography of Margaret Hill written in 1978, by kind permission of her family, which gives a first-hand account of the development of the Trust from many of those involved; and from more recent years we have press cuttings, journal articles and photos to supplement the archive. We don't know what we don't know. But what we can find out is still interesting.

Rosie Boughton, July 2023

Foreword

In 2023 we celebrate our 90th anniversary. In the spring of 1933 our founder, Margaret Hill, set up the Trust and persuaded Hornsey Borough Council to lend the money to buy three houses in Hornsey, and then 47 more before the onset of World War 2. As a local councillor, she was only too aware of the housing issues in the area and, with the support of a group of fellow pioneers, established the Trust funded with a combination of loans from the Borough, private loans and donations. Ninety years on, we own 391 homes specialising in housing mostly single people over the age of 45 in need of a decent home that they can afford. The average age of a Trust tenant is currently 70.

We haven't strayed far from our origins, providing homes exclusively in the London Borough of Haringey, formed when the Municipal Boroughs of Hornsey, Tottenham, and Wood Green merged in 1965. Indeed, most of our homes are still in Hornsey though we also have some in Tottenham and Wood Green. We are fortunate that Rosie Boughton, a former board member of the Trust and its chair until 2020, decided to write this fascinating history to help us celebrate an important milestone. She is one of many women who have been board members over the years and the significant involvement of women is one of the themes that comes out of this history.

Throughout the life of the Trust, many board members have had a connection to the Hornsey area and been driven by a commitment to providing good quality housing for local people, regardless of income. Originally, this included family housing, but from quite early on the Trust has focussed on the needs of older people. However, the Trust has always wanted to provide 'more than just housing'. In its early days, it responded to people's personal circumstances – from sending a couple on holiday when the husband had been ill, to providing a live-in matron in shared houses for elderly people. Up until the early 21st Century, we still provided care for our tenants in our sheltered housing. As funding has changed, however, we have had to refocus our efforts on ensuring our tenants can access care from other providers and also maximise their state entitlements. We help new tenants get furniture and floor coverings when they move, if needed; and try and provide a range of social activities to tackle the loneliness and isolation that has increasingly affected our ageing population.

We are currently looking at what we want to achieve in the next 10 years, so that we have more to celebrate on our 100th anniversary. We have some major challenges – improving our existing homes to make them more resilient as our climate changes, and to reduce their carbon impact and their running costs for our tenants and the Trust. We want to build new homes – we have ambitions for more than 20 during this period, replacing existing properties that are going to be too expensive or difficult to upgrade and enabling our tenants to move to a better home.

We need to continue to focus on ensuring our finances are robust – Margaret Hill left us with great assets but our annual income is relatively low because of our size, and our continuing commitment to keep rents genuinely affordable.

Finally, the history of the Trust is also the story of our tenants; you will get a sense of who they have been over the years from this book. We are now refocussing our approach to running the Trust in partnership with our tenants, so we respond where we can to their needs and ambitions; so they better understand our constraints – financial and otherwise; and so we ensure that the decisions we take make sense for both our current and our future tenants. Meanwhile we continue to hold our assets in trust for the use of local people.

My thanks go to Rosie for her work on this history and I hope you all enjoy reading the book as much as I have.

June Barnes, Chair of Hornsey Housing Trust
July 2023

Setting the scene

Hornsey Housing Trust owes its existence to one person, Margaret Hill. She founded it in 1933, and nurtured it through its first 25 years. Her conviction was that *'the underlying cause of much discomfort, ill-health and unhappiness in many families was the bad conditions of their houses'* (CR1 1935), and she decided to do something about that. She was the right person in the right place at the right time.

Hornsey in the 1930s
In the 1930s, Hornsey's housing stock was not old. Most of it had been built quite recently, in late Victorian and Edwardian times, as part of the general expansion of London facilitated by the building of the railways. The train made it possible to commute to work in central London, and then return home to a larger house, less crowded streets, cleaner air and greener spaces: the two trees on the coat of arms of 'Healthy Hornsey' as it was known, referred back to the ancient forests which used to occupy the slopes of the Northern Heights. The houses in Hornsey had been built for the middle classes: solidly constructed, often with four or five bedrooms, assuming that the household would employ – and accommodate – one or more servants. Census records show how the population of Hornsey grew, from 11,000 in 1861 to 85,000 in 1911.

The First World War came close to Hornsey's doorstep. In 1914 Alexandra Palace was commissioned for use by Belgian refugees, and was then used as an internment camp for over 1,000 German nationals. The 1920s then saw major changes on a national level, which impacted the whole country. A faltering national economy led to widespread unemployment, culminating in the General Strike of 1926; and three years later the Wall Street Crash heralded the start of the Depression, a time of unemployment and poverty for many more. Social changes were also in progress: during the War, many women had been employed outside domestic service for the first time to take the place of men joining the armed forces; and post-War, the gender imbalance consequent on the loss of so many men meant fewer marriages and more women continuing in work.

What would it have been like to live in Hornsey then? Inside the home, coal fires provided heating, though electricity and gas were now becoming available for cooking and lighting. Domestic fridges were not yet used, so fresh food had to be bought more often. Residents with no washing facilities were expected to use the public bath and wash houses in Priory Road – even the new council houses built by the Borough Council in the 1920s had no separate bathrooms, just a bath with a wooden lid in the kitchen.

Outside the home, there were few private cars yet, and many roads (like Muswell Hill Road) were still gravelled. The mature trees we see lining the streets today would have been saplings. Though much of Hornsey was residential, many businesses were located here:

> 'A sizeable working population were engaged in service work, such as shops, laundries and in a number of small manufacturing establishments. These included piano and organ factories, sweets and chocolate manufacture, light engineering and small workshops. Long hours, hard work and low wages were common. But Hornsey was a diverse community which engendered strong local loyalties.' (Gay, 1988)

Meanwhile, all around, building continued. Much of this was for residential housing on undeveloped land – north of Fortis Green for example, or on the few remaining big estates such as Elm House in Middle Lane. However, the early 1930s also saw the construction of several landmark buildings familiar to us today – Park Road Lido (1929), Muswell Hill Library (1932), the Everyman Cinema (1935), and Hornsey Town Hall and the trade buildings in front of it (1935 – 1937).

Hornsey Town Hall and environs, Crouch End, 1938 (EPW059124).
This image has been produced from a copy-negative. © Historic England

In 1936 the first BBC television programmes were beamed out from Alexandra Palace.

Hornsey Borough Council

The precursor to Hornsey Borough Council, Hornsey Local Board, was set up in the nineteenth century to manage the supply of water and sewerage, the removal of rubbish, and the maintenance of highways. This developed into Hornsey Borough Council in 1903, meeting in its old town hall in Southwood Lane. It seems to have been quite forward looking, generating its own electricity in Tottenham Lane from 1903, and using clinker residue to make asphalt to surface its roads. It was also early to build council houses, and by 1913, had built over 400, including the Nightingale Lane Estate and surrounding streets – more than any other Greater London borough (Denford, 2008). At the end of the First World War, alarmed by the Russian revolution of 1917 and aware of its squads of young soldiers returning to the UK, the government instituted a programme of 'Homes Fit for Heroes', and Hornsey was one of the first to take up the new funding made available, building the Coldfall Estate in Coppetts Road.

It's from Hornsey Borough Council's Medical Officer of Health that we get a detailed description of housing in the Borough in 1922. He said that there were 'no slum areas'; however, there were real problems of overcrowding and high rents:

> 'Many houses in the Borough which were originally intended and built for the use of one family are now occupied by two or more families, and it is in these especially that sanitary supervision is needed. If two, three or four families share a sink or water-closet, it is no one's business to keep it clean: it is the business of nobody to look after the common passage and the common back-yard.

> 'Another evil associated with the subletting of these houses is that many of the families have no proper cooking-place: there is only one cooking range or gas-cooker in the house, and only one family has access to it. The remainder have to get along as best they can by cooking on a bedroom fire or on a gas-ring. Hot water and baths are unknown luxuries in many of these tenements, and it is not to be wondered at that vermin are sometimes found in these houses. Indeed, it is a matter for astonishment that so many people in such adverse circumstances manage to keep themselves and their homes clean and respectable .I do not think that the provision of more working-class houses would materially diminish this overcrowding, for the reason that the families now living in one or two rooms could not afford to live in larger houses and to pay an additional rent'.
> (quoted in Hornsey Historical Society Newsletter 173)

Social support in the 1930s

In any community there are some who cannot earn an income to support themselves. This may be temporary – during unemployment, for example, or a bout of ill health. Or it may be a more lasting matter, such as disability or the frailty of old age. For some centuries – since the 1601 Poor Law – supporting such people was the responsibility of the local church parish. Workhouses were built, often by a 'union' of several parishes, to provide subsistence support, sometimes in exchange for unpaid work. Since 1837, Hornsey parish had been part of the union using Edmonton workhouse – where North Middlesex

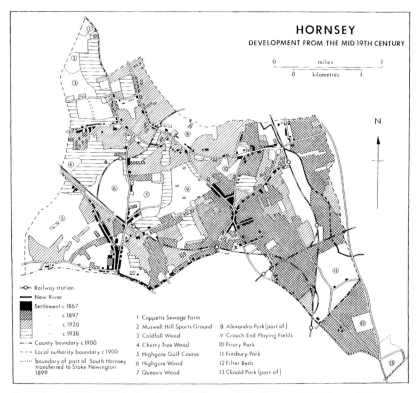

Reproduced with permission from '*A History of the County of Middlesex: Volume 6, Friern Barnet, Finchley, Hornsey with Highgate*', Victoria County History, London 1980 © University of London

Hospital is now sited – and still maintained 66 people there in 1903. The union workhouses were supervised by Boards of Guardians, elected by local ratepayers.

However, the support provided by parishes was inconsistent, and often intentionally demeaning. Before and after the First World War there was much debate in England about how to improve such support. Many, like Beatrice and Sydney Webb (social reformers who founded the London School of Economics) took the view that the state should take on the responsibility of providing a national minimum standard of living. Some changes were made by governments: an old age pension was introduced in 1908 for those over 70, a national health insurance scheme in 1911, and unemployment insurance in 1920. And then in 1930, the responsibility for poor relief was taken away from workhouses and their Boards of Guardians. It was given instead to Public Assistance Committees (PACs) answerable to local councils, and the local Guardians' Committees who reported to them. A Means Test was introduced in 1931, and then in 1934 Unemployment Assistance Boards (UACs) took over the assessment of benefit entitlements for those without work.

How much support was offered? George Orwell provides a lot of detail about how much a household might receive, and in what circumstances, in 'The Road to Wigan Pier' (1937). However, it is hard to relate amounts of money then to sums now. For a sense of what living on public assistance was like, the fictional excerpt below from Nevil Shute's novel Ruined City (1938) may help:

> *'There's really nothing wrong with the rates of relief. If you are careful, and wise, and prudent, you can live on that amount of money fairly well. And you've got to be intelligent, and well educated too, and rather selfish. If you were like that, you'd get along all right – but you wouldn't have a penny to spare. But if you were human – well you'd be for it. If you got bored stiff with*

doing nothing so that you went and blued fourpence on going to the pictures – you just wouldn't have enough to eat that week. Or if you couldn't cook very well, and spoiled the food a bit, you'd go hungry.'

The principle behind the workhouse system, and persisting through the PAC/UAC system, was that it was necessary to distinguish between the 'deserving' and the 'undeserving' poor, a notion which first surfaced legally in the 1834 Poor Law. This holds that support from the wider community should be reserved for those who are poor through no fault of their own. As a consequence, although the workhouses were open to all, they were deliberately designed to provide a very basic subsistence level of support, to ensure that those who could work if they chose, would choose to do so. Applicants to the PAC and UAC would find that they needed to explain how and why they needed support, to a Committee with wide discretion about the sums they awarded: the experience is well set out in Winifred Holtby's novel 'South Riding' (1936). Indeed, the notion that social support should be kept at a minimal level in order not to encourage idleness and fecklessness is alive today.

Margaret Hill

Margaret Hill later said it was her experience as a Poor Law Guardian which led to her founding Hornsey Housing Trust. The *'situation was brought clearly before me as a Guardian, when I did a considerable amount of visiting and saw how pensioners had to put up with the cheapest possible accommodation, usually an attic or a damp basement room.'* (Hill, 1961). She was first elected a councillor on Hornsey Borough Council in 1929, and remained a councillor, and then an alderman, for the next 19 years. As we will see, the close relationship between the Trust and the Borough Council had a lot to do with the successful development of the Trust, and her role was critical to that. However, her exposure to the practicalities of public service, and the debates surrounding it, had started at a much younger age.

Margaret Hill was born Margaret Keynes, into an academic family in Cambridge, in 1885. Both her brothers achieved national and international renown, John Maynard as an economist and Geoffrey as a surgeon and scholar. But it may have been her mother's role which had most influence on her. Florence, a graduate of Newnham College, Cambridge, was active in social reform projects in the city, and became the first female councillor on Cambridge City Council in 1914, and eventually Lord Mayor. Margaret wrote much later:

> *'As a child living in a household where such things were discussed and hearing my mother talk about her practical work, I was continually astonished that, apparently, it was thought a disgraceful thing to be poor.....People in workhouses seemed to*

Margaret Hill in her garden in Highgate, 1936; by kind permission of Nicholas Humphrey

me to be undergoing a kind of punishment – punishment for being dependent on others – and I often heard it said that conditions must not be too pleasant or more people would seek the same kind of assistance, thus throwing a great burden on the community.' (Hill, 1961)

Margaret herself did not go to university; her first formal role was as secretary of the Boys' Employment Registry in Cambridge, set up in 1907 to identify training, apprenticeship and job opportunities for boys when they left school. A key relationship which she developed there was with Eglantyne Jebb, who went on to found the charity Save the Children. In 1913 she married AV Hill, an eminent physiologist, and in 1923 they moved to London for him to take up a new professorial post at University College, and settled in Bishopswood Road, Highgate, where they lived for the next 40 years and brought up their four children.

In 1925, her children now at school, Margaret helped set up Hornsey Borough Council's third Maternity and Child Welfare Centre in Highgate. This led to her co-option on to the Council's Maternity and Child Welfare Committee two years later. And then in 1929, when a by-election was held in Highgate Ward, she stood as an Independent candidate, and was elected a Hornsey Borough councillor. In addition to her Council responsibilities, she joined the executive committee of the Hornsey District Nursing Association, and the Hornsey branch of the National Council of Women.

According to her biographer, it was likely that it was this last organisation which provided Margaret with a housing model to follow (Angier, 1978). In 1926 the Cambridge branch – of which her mother was still an active member – had set up the Cambridge Women's Housing Association, to buy large houses for conversion to flats; in this it was successful, although limited in its scope as it was reliant for its funding on private loans. Similar initiatives were followed by other branches in the next few years – in Bromley, Malvern, York, Coventry, Hull and London. Margaret's work with the Highgate Welfare Centre, as a Guardian, with the District Nursing Association and as a councillor on Hornsey's Housing Committee would have familiarised her with the extent of housing need in Hornsey, and would also have provided her with an invaluable understanding of local organisational networks and resources. In 1933, then, she set up Hornsey Housing Trust, which she chaired for the next twenty-five years.

Early growth: 1933–1939

On April 26th 1933, Hornsey Housing Trust was registered as a Public Utility Company under the Industrial and Provident Societies legislation (No.11578R London). At the first meeting of its Committee of Management the day after, Margaret Hill was elected Chairman. The minutes of that meeting mainly dwell on the formal business of setting up a new organisation, but also tell us that Margaret Hill and her friend Lady Waley Cohen had already contracted to buy two houses – 10 Pembroke Road and 101 Nelson Road.

The Trust's objectives were set out in the Chairman's report to the 1935 AGM:

> 'It was realized in Hornsey, though this cannot be claimed as an original or novel idea, that the underlying cause of much discomfort, ill-health and unhappiness in many families was the bad conditions of their houses. Continually cases were found in which the domestic difficulties were at the bottom of social evils. High rents, intolerably cramped conditions, uncongenial neighbours, complete absence of suitable amenities, all made life for many people a continual and unnecessary struggle.
>
> In this district, as in many others, the outcome of this realization was the formation of a Public Utility Society, the object of which was to buy old houses and adapt them for the use of more than the one family for which they were originally designed at the lowest possible rents, on an economic basis.'

Finance

The funding for the Trust's work was to come from two main sources: the first was investment by the general public though the purchase of shares or loan stock. The issuing of loan stock was a customary measure by 19th century housing trusts – sometimes referred to as

'5% philanthropy'. The investor would lend money to the Trust on the basis of a return which was at a lower rate than could be gained elsewhere. The organisation would then have the capital it needed to buy and improve homes, and would generate a return for the investors from the rent. The earliest loan stock prospectus we have for the Trust is from 1934, but further requests were made in the following years.

The much more significant source of funding, however, was Hornsey Borough Council, and this is where Hornsey Housing Trust may have broken new ground. Councils themselves could borrow money from the government at low rates of interest; but then under the Housing Act 1925, they were empowered to lend this money on similar terms to organisations such as housing trusts. Margaret Hill – Councillor Hill – seems to have been the first to perceive the potential of this legislation, and Hornsey Housing Trust the first to benefit from it. Once the Trust had a legal entity, it sought a loan agreement with the Borough Council, and it was soon reported that this had been achieved: the Borough Council agreed *'advances...on the security of any properties which the Trust may acquire of sums not exceeding 85% of the improved value'* (CM 28/6/33). (Some conditions were attached: in particular, the Council had to approve the purchase price; and leaseholds needed to have a minimum of 60 years to run.)

The Trust was not slow to use the benefit of this agreement in its search for supplementary private funding: the 1934 Loan Stock prospectus underlines the point: *'The Low Rents, are to a large extend (sic) made possible by the fact that 85% of the money required can be borrowed from the Borough Council.... Thus £15 subscribed makes £100 available.'* It was in the interests of both organisations to make good use of this provision as their work was to be complementary: the Borough clearing land and building new estates, the Trust buying and repurposing existing homes.

At its first meeting, the Committee agreed to set up an 'Advisory

Request for Loan Stock 1933

Applications for Shares or Loan Stock are invited by The Hornsey Housing Trust. The housing situation in the district could be definitely improved for the poorer members of the community if adequate support to the Scheme were given by those in better circumstances.

The Executive Committee has among its members an Architect, a Surveyor, a Builder and an Accountant who give much voluntary service in an endeavour to provide Flats at the lowest rents compatible with a return of 31/2% on the Loan Stock and a dividend (max 4%) on the money subscribed.

The Low Rents, are to a large extend made possible by the fact that 85% of the money required can be borrowed from the Borough Council at £3. 12. 6. % Thus £15 subscribed makes £100 available. The Trust in its short life of 9 months has provided accommodation for about 80 individuals and can go steadily forward as further funds are made available.

Two families are being moved from single rooms. In both cases the standard of cleanliness and order was amazingly high and the reason for the overcrowding as a small income due to unavoidable causes.

In three cases families were moved because, on account of the illness of the wage-earner, they were paying rents which absorbed so large a proportion of the Incomes that definite undernourishment resulted. The three families are all enjoying improved accommodation for an average weekly reduction of 7/4 each on their rents. One object of the Trust is to provide suitable accommodation for middle class people who, through misfortune, have to seek much cheaper accommodation than they have been accustomed to. The Committee has already been able to help two old age pensioners *whose brother exhibited at the Royal Academy for 25 years and whose father was also an artist. These refined old people were living in conditions, verging on squalor and now, for the same rent, have a small flat fitted with every convenience.*

Altogether ten Old Pensioners are being housed and in all cases their present accommodation is very much more suited to their age and infirmity than that vacated. If it were realised that many old people of 70–80 years of age have to carry all their water and coals up one or more flights of stairs the means of relieving them would surely be forthcoming.

From the present experience gained the Committee are confident that with suitable management on Octavia Hill Lines much help of a permanent and in no sense demoralising nature can be afforded to a large number of people. They wish to emphasize that they are not asking for gifts but inviting subscriptions at a reasonable rate of interest.

Transcribed from loan stock prospectus, Hornsey Housing Trust archive

Council', including the Mayor of Hornsey, and Margaret Hill's brother John Maynard Keynes. By 1935 this comprised 14 illustrious names, including a peer of the realm, a member of parliament, two justices of the peace, and the Rector of Hornsey. What functions the Advisory Council performed are unknown to us, but these names would be likely to reassure those from whom the Trust was seeking investment.

Committee of Management

The Trust started its activities energetically, acquiring and 'reconditioning' three properties in its first nine months, and a further seventeen the following year. The minutes show that a good deal of the Committee's attention was on financial matters: new applications for shares and loan stock; insurance; rents; contracts to refurbish the houses which had been purchased. Should the Trust equip houses with electric light, and if so, should tenants bear part of the cost? Some decision-making was delegated to the Chairman, whether securing and approving estimates for works, or applying for loans to the Borough Council. This even extended to new purchases: in November 1934 '*The Committee authorised the Chairman and Treasurer to buy two more houses, if suitable ones could be found, before the next meeting*' (CM 29/11/34).

Attention was paid to what was called 'propaganda' – publicising the work of the Trust to attract more investors. A music recital is mentioned and a bridge tournament, when Margaret Hill would speak about the Trust at the interval, and share application forms would be laid on the seats. Meetings were held with prominent speakers – John Maynard Keynes, at a 'Drawing Room Meeting' held by Lady Waley Cohen at her home (now Athlone House), and later on, Lord Balfour: both meetings were reported in detail in the local press. Interested parties were invited to see a property – 39 Burgoyne Road – once it had been converted.

The membership of the Committee of Management remained broadly the same through this period – indeed until after the Second World War – and Margaret Hill remained Chairman throughout. This will have provided a welcome level of consistency through these early years. During this time, two people joined the Trust who would play an important role during wartime and for several decades after. One was her great friend Norah Clegg (who also wrote the lively minutes of the Tenants' Assistance Fund); as an early member of the Committee of Management later said: '*Margaret Hill was the father of the Trust, and Norah Clegg its mother*' (Angier 1978). The other was Len Belfall, who joined the Trust as a plumber and general builder, and stayed for over 40 years.

The Chairman's Report at the Annual General Meeting, on March 27th, 1934.

›···The tenants have not been chosen on account of their ability to pay their rents, which is the chief concern of most landlords, but on account of their need. They include unemployed men, cripples, old age pensioners, chronic invalids, a deserted woman and several middle class families who have fallen on evil days. It is therefore all the more satisfactory that there are *no* arrears of rent.

The surveying, planning of alterations, secretarial work and rent collecting are all done voluntarily, so that the working expenses are reduced to a minimum. The Trust is very greatly indebted to those who give their professional knowledge and a large amount of their leisure to the work. The work of the Treasurer is unending and really arduous. The Secretary also never has a free day. Lastly, the women rent collectors ensure the permanent success of the scheme: it is no good moving people into flats of this kind and then taking no further notice of them. Miss Octavia Hill realized this many years ago, and this side of the work of the Trust is run on broadly the same principles as she laid down. We are most fortunate in having several ladies on the Committee who are willing to undertake this most necessary and responsible task.

No account of the first year's work would be complete without reference to the invaluable help and advice which has been given by the Town Clerk of Hornsey, and to the friendly co-operation of other Officials from the Sanitary, the Surveyors and the Borough Treasurer's Departments, whose help is necessarily sought in connection with the buying and re-conditioning of the houses on which the Borough makes loans of 85 per cent. of their value.

A Subsidiary Committee has also been formed, known as the Tenants' Assistance Committe: this deals with many of the needs of the tenants which fall outside the province of the Trust itself. Thanks to the generosity of Lady Waley Cohen, who lent her house for the purpose, a Bridge and a Whist Drive were held which resulted in the sum of about £180 to form the nucleus of a fund for necessary loans, convalescence, expenses of moving, and many other purposes.····

Extract from the Chairman's Report to the first AGM of Hornsey Housing Trust, March 27th 1934 (Hornsey Housing Trust archive)

The first houses

By the time war broke out, the Trust had bought 50 houses. Of course, one property did not equate to one tenancy: the crude equation, looking at the figures below, is that each property accommodated four or five tenancies, and around ten people.

Year (AGM)	Properties	Tenancies			People
		1–2 people	3–10 people	All	
1933	3	–	–	–	–
1934	17	–	–	–	–
1935	28	–	–	91	312
1936	34	–	–	127	372
1937	41	113	62	175	416
1938	46	160	48	208	415
1939	50	176	48	237	423

Compiled from AGM and Chairman's reports

The Chairman's report to the first Annual General Meeting on March 27th 1934, sets out the circumstances of the 27 households which the Trust had already rehoused in its first year of operation. This gives a good idea of the difficult housing circumstances of many at the time, for example:

> 'The first family to be moved into a new flat came from Muswell Hill Road. There were five children and their parents, and their living room measured 13 ft by 9 ft. They had one bedroom and shortly before the move the eldest child had died of a rheumatic heart. It was not possible for all the family to sit down at once for meals and the discomfort was great. The seven of them now occupy three bedrooms and a good kitchen which opens into a dry yard.'

And more succinctly:
5. *Five people moved from poor flat to better accommodation at 5s 6d less rent weekly*
6. *Two old age pensioners moved to better rooms at reduction of 2s 6d weekly in rent*
25. *Parents and six young adults moved from two rooms, their lives will be much more pleasant in a self-contained five roomed flat*

A Hornsey Housing Trust flatlet. Reproduced from a photograph in 'An Approach to Old Age and its Problems', Margaret Hill, 1961.

How were these houses organised? Where there were several tenancies in a house, these would rarely have been in self-contained accommodation as we understand it today, that is a flat which included bed and living rooms, kitchen and bathroom, with its own front door. Toilets, and bathrooms where they existed, were usually shared, though the Trust tried to ensure that each flat had its own kitchen and water supply. There was some flexibility, in consequence, about how many rooms each tenant occupied, with scope for a family to give up a room (if children moved out) or to gain an extra room if they grew in size. There was also, inevitably, scope for friction between tenants: coal was stolen, more electricity was used by one household than another, personalities clashed. Dealing with all these day-to-day housing management issues was the responsibility of the Tenants' Assistance Fund Committee.

Tenants' Assistance Fund
The Tenants' Assistance Fund (TAF) was set up early in the life of the Trust, in 1933. We have two hand-written minute books which record the meetings of the Fund Committee, one 1935 – 1940, the other 1940–1953. Throughout, Margaret Hill acted as Chairman, and the meetings were held at her house. For most of these years, the members of the TAF Committee – almost all women – voluntarily managed the Trust's tenancies, visiting every tenant every week to collect the rent, and keeping closely in touch with their tenants' lives, engaging in what would today be described as social work. In this, they explicitly followed the model of housing management developed by Octavia Hill in the 19th century. Octavia Hill (no relation) was a social reformer who developed housing management as a profession, based on the principle that *'You cannot deal with the people and their houses separately'* (englishheritage.org.uk). She took a wide view of a landlord's responsibilities towards its tenants, but insisted on tenants discharging their responsibilities too, especially in respect of paying the rent on time. Today's professional housing body, the Chartered Institute of Housing, evolved from her practice.

In the first six years, the Trust's TAF Committee met monthly, and discussed perhaps 15–20 of the houses and tenancies each time: the new houses which had been bought, who they had been let to, when rooms might be allocated differently in a house, and the health and wellbeing of the tenants – as well as when arrears had arisen, or disputes erupted. The minutes display an intimate familiarity with the lives of the Trust's tenants. A few examples:

> *'Miss S is to move into 77 Middle Lane – top 2 back rooms at 11/- a week. Mrs C is to go into Miss S's flat and the Bs are going into Mrs C's flat.'* (TA1 17/2/37)
>
> *'84 Rathcoole Gardens: Mrs B goes out to work now, and Mrs H looks after all 10 children and gets their dinners ready and is given 6d per day by Mrs B, for which she is very grateful'* (TA1 15/10/37)
>
> *'19 Hillfield Avenue: All are quarrelling here again as usual'* (TA1 18/1/39)
>
> *'(Mr) P is going rapidly downhill. Mrs Hill sent him to hospital to be overhauled. The report was 'undernourished and incapable of work' so he will get more money on sick pay'* (TA1 18/1/39)

A key function of the TAF was paying for a range of benefits to tenants – though cash was not directly provided. The Committee seems to have had a broad discretion about what they spent money on; mentioned are, among other things:

- *Health* – medicine, spectacles, 'extra nourishment' for a sick pregnant woman; cod liver oil; a seaside break after illness
- *Furniture* – lino, beds, commode for bedridden, small greenhouse, blankets, gas fire (sometimes in the form of a loan, repaid over time with the rent)
- *Home helps* for temporary periods
- *Fuel* – coal through the winter at 1 cwt a week
- *Rent* – an occasional week's rent to pay off small arrears
- *Paying off debts* – eg for furniture on hire purchase
- *Fares* – for a tenant looking for work

> 'Mrs S is going into hospital at the end of this week to have another baby and she was very worried about her 2 babies – so we have arranged for a home help to go in every day for the 10 days or fortnight while she is away. The cost is 25/- a week, the Ss are to pay 5/- and the TAF £1 per week.' (TA1 17/3/37)

> 'Mr B has been a week in arrears owing to his accident so the TAF have given him 12/6d to bring his rent book up to date' (TA1 14/12/37)

> 'Mr M has been very ill so the TAF decided to send him to Canvey Island for a fortnight's change of air' (TA1 19/1/39)

The TAF was also responsible for occasional treats – Christmas presents (tea, sweets, Christmas cakes) and sometimes a party. A 1938 newspaper cutting writes up a 'Merry Afternoon at the Town Hall' at which Margaret Hill's two sons provided entertainment. And in 1939, a Garden Party was held, for which the rent collectors were asked to submit lists of tenants who might be invited (TA 15/6/39). Occasionally they considered a life-changing issue:

> 'Mrs Hill had been asked if she knew of a suitable boy to emigrate to the Fairbridge Farm School, New Zealand. S was proposed. He is a handsome well grown boy, and seems to be intelligent, but has a poor miserable mother who cannot control him at all, and the home is made unhappy by incessant nagging and scolding. The father is dead.' (TA1 23/9/35)

Where did the money come from? Several sources are described in the minute books: a sale of clothes at Caledonian Market; sale of sweets; whist drive; Bring and Buy at Mrs Hill's house; and donations (for instance £100 from Margaret Hill's brother John Maynard Keynes;

£50 from Lady Darwin of Cambridge). In 1936, the Committee of Management agreed that a 4% dividend on the value of any donations should be paid to the TAF, which provided a steady source of income.

Doing harm by doing good?
In the early years of the Trust, Margaret Hill more than once defended the provision of such assistance, suggesting that she had encountered criticism of it. For example, in her short pamphlet '*An Experiment in Housing*' (1934) she wrote:

> 'It has been argued that such help as has been afforded will inevitably lead to an unsatisfactory relationship between landlord and tenant. Actually the reverse has been found to be the case. There are no arrears of rent and the tenants have, without exception, responded to their improved conditions.
>
> ...an example of the kind of problem to be met is that of a man in regular but poorly paid work who lived with his wife and five children in two rooms with no cooking arrangement, besides an open, smoky grate, no water laid on and no separate conveniences of any kind. To move this family into a larger flat without the Tenants' Assistance Fund would have meant inability to pay for the removal, uncovered floors and an insufficient number of beds unless they had recourse to borrowing, by virtue of the hire-purchase system.'

And again, in her Chairman's report of 1935:

> 'The working of this fund has been found more satisfactory than was anticipated by some who felt it to be treading on dangerous ground and likely to undermine the sense of responsibility of the poorer tenants. In actual experience the response has far exceeded expectation. In no case has this treatment resulted in the proverbial asking for more, and there has never been a week's rent in arrears.'

That said, the Committee was aware that there were boundaries to be kept:

> 'It was decided that the rent collectors be requested not to visit tenants without notice – unless requested to do so – or in special cases of illness. It is essential that their independence as tenants be respected' (TA1 13/1/37).

Letters to the Editor

Re-Modelling Houses

OLD BUILDINGS AND NEW FLATS

From Councillor Mrs. A. V. HILL, Chairman, Hornsey Housing Trust Ltd.

To the Editor of "The Daily Telegraph and Morning Post"

Sir—You state in your leading article of Oct. 20 that much useful work in remodelling existing houses is being done by housing societies, and that there is much force in the suggestion that grants should be available for this purpose.

It is not generally known that it is possible for local authorities to lend up to 90 per cent. of the value of reconditioned houses at a low rate of interest to housing societies. This plan has been adopted in Hornsey, and has enabled a local housing trust to adapt existing houses for the use of people needing accommodation of one or two rooms.

This has been done much more cheaply and in many cases more satisfactorily than could have been done by demolishing and rebuilding. One of the advantages which is often overlooked is the absence of isolation which the old often feel in new blocks of flats, and which is in many cases almost as burdensome as the opposite extreme of institutional life.

There is considerable local pride and community feeling in well ordered flatlet houses which comes nearer to the neighbourliness existing in streets of small houses and now being rapidly lost in large blocks of flats.

The problem of housing the old is growing rapidly. In 1900 there were 1,750,000 persons over 65 years of age; in 1931 there were over 3,000,000, and in 1941 there will probably be another 1,000,000 added. This is a part of the problem to which housing societies may find they will need to devote more attention.

I should like to make a further point. The interesting character of a good many towns will be lost to future generations if the majority of the larger well-built houses of the past, which have outlived their original purpose, continue to be ruthlessly destroyed in favour of large and often unsightly blocks of flats. From every point of view let us preserve them before it is too late for the use and enjoyment of many people.—Yours, faithfully, M. N. HILL.
16, Bishopswood-road, N. 6. Oct. 22.

Letter to the Daily Telegraph from Margaret Hill, October 1938

Quite apart from the work of the Tenants' Assistance Fund in distributing benefits, Margaret Hill was very clear that the primary job of the Trust in offering decent housing at a price people could afford, was in her view an unequivocal good:

> 'There is no reason, even now, why an old pensioner should carry water and coal up several flights of stairs and submit, generally uncomplainingly, to the most cheerless and uncomfortable surroundings. There is no hint of demoralization or of lack of independence produced by such help. It damages nobody's character to pay less rent, to have more rooms, with a larder, a sink and a tap.' (CR 1935)

Who did Hornsey Housing Trust house?

What choices did Hornsey Housing Trust make in those early years about who they housed? We know something of the housing circumstances of the earliest tenants from the examples given above. Curiously, this is not an issue discussed in terms of a general policy in the Committee of Management. In respect of a specific property it was at one point agreed that *'the selection of tenants be left to the Chairman'* (CM 18/1/35). And later, when a Daily Mail article resulted in a flood of applications, they were *'duly forwarded to the Chairman for her to deal with'* (CM 18/6/36). A later reference suggests that date order of application was a relevant factor, but there was clearly a degree of discretion exercised about who was offered a tenancy. Later in her life Margaret Hill wrote:

> 'The original idea was to house those whom we found living in the most deplorable conditions, both old people and very poor families. This policy nearly wrecked the scheme, because those who were in the greatest need were frequently the least dependable and the least capable of paying their rent...As time went on, our policy in choosing tenants was changed. Gradually we came to know of the existence of many excellent people, especially the old, who endeavoured to hide their poverty but had known better days.' (Hill, 1961)

Pragmatically, for the Trust to survive and prosper, it had to be able to pay back its loans; it needed tenants who would pay their rent.

A developing focus on older tenants

It is evident from the documentation we have, that even in these early years there was an increasing interest from the Trust in the housing needs of older tenants. In her Chairman's report of 1938, Margaret Hill expands on *'The Problem of Housing the Old'*, for whom the options are often limited to living with relatives, renting a room in someone else's house, or entering institutional care. By this time, the Trust was letting over 100 flatlets for older people, each with private space for the tenant and their possessions, amenities such as individual water supply, sinks and warmth; and providing *'the comfort of a permanent home'* together with *'being once more part of a small community'*, with *'removal of one fear as to what the future will bring'*. She wrote that *'the demand for these flatlets is insatiable'*.

In this report she explicitly states that there has been a change of policy within the organisation, away from housing families and towards housing older people. A number of reasons are given for this: the success of the work of the Borough Council in reducing overcrowding in Hornsey; the increase in life expectancy leading to an increase in the numbers of older people; and the greater ease with which the large family houses in Hornsey could be converted into smaller flatlets for one or two people rather than larger flats for families. Housing for older people was becoming a particular interest for her. She would have encountered many older people experiencing problems with their housing during her time as a Guardian (a majority of applicants were incapacitated by old age); and also through her work with the Highgate Welfare Centre, and the Hornsey District Nursing Association.

The greater priority given to housing older tenants was accompanied by an understanding at the Trust that some older people may need additional support in order to continue to live independently. As we have seen, the Tenants' Assistance Fund already paid for home helps from time to time, but a more permanent solution needed to be found for a handful of tenants. In June 1939, a supported home was opened at 47 Cecile Park, for eight residents, with a manager, a daily cook, and a weekly visit from a nurse to assist in bathing. It was called Delia Grotten's House, after its first resident, a retired matron from the police service, and was largely funded by the County Council. There was such demand for its provision, that within the year it had moved to 14 Mountview Road, where it could accommodate 20 residents.

The achievements of these early years
In these first six years, Hornsey Housing Trust grew from an idea, to an organisation providing decent housing for over 400 people. 50 houses had been purchased, and then repaired and adapted for the convenient use of over 200 households. Waiting list applicants had been interviewed and settled into their new homes, the TAF volunteers had been allocated their rent collection rounds, private investment had been sought and found, fundraising events organised, and the productive relationship with the Borough Council nurtured. And in 1937, the decision was taken that the Trust should apply to become a charity. Much – perhaps most – of this work had been done by Margaret Hill, and it seems she enjoyed it. She later commented approvingly on the speed at which they could work: *'no plans had to be sent for inspection, no delays were caused by Ministries, and hampering bye-laws were few'* (Hill, 1961). The job that needed to be done suited her abilities and preferences very well: her energy, her pragmatic approach, her ability to inspire others, and to harness the contributions of others towards the Trust's objectives.

The war years: 1939–1945

Living through the war in Hornsey

The outbreak of World War Two changed the work of the Trust in many ways. Despite its distance from central London, Hornsey experienced a good deal of bomb damage during the war, particularly during the Blitz in the winter of 1940/41; and then again in 1944 with the advent of V1 flying bombs and V2 rockets. In the Borough as a whole, over 700 homes were lost, either destroyed or damaged so badly they had to be demolished. The Trust's housing stock was no exception. Though only one dwelling was completely destroyed, during the hostilities 43 of the Trust's 50 houses were damaged, some more than once: one house in Park Avenue South had to be repaired five times.

Tottenham Lane and Ribblesdale Road showing damage to Ribblesdale Road following V2 incident November 1944, by permission of Bruce Castle Museum (Haringey Archive and Museum Service).

Occasionally, several of its houses suffered bomb damage at the same time – on one day in 1944, 11 houses were damaged in Hillfield Avenue and Ferrestone Road; on another, six houses in Cecile Park were hit by incendiary bombs. It is thought that the railway line around Hornsey Station may have been a particular target.

'60 and 62 Denton Road have been hit by a bomb and very badly damaged – none of the tenants were hurt. 46 Denton also was damaged by blast…the Fs have been temporarily house(d) in 55 Hillfield Avenue and are returning to 46 Denton when it has been repaired.' (TA2 17/9/40)

Thankfully, no serious casualties are mentioned among the Trust's tenants, though in the Borough as a whole, over 200 civilians lost their lives, and a further 1,200 were injured.

The changes to Hornsey residents' lives would have been significant. All learned to use shelters, especially at night: in the first year, Anderson shelters were dug in private gardens, to accommodate most Borough residents, and 'trench' shelters were dug in many public open spaces for a further 10,000. Over 4,000 people routinely spent the night on the platforms of Highgate Underground Station. Several thousand residents, a quarter of them women, volunteered to join the Civil Defence – fire-watching, patrolling and offering first aid. Some families were evacuated, and others chose to leave London because of anxiety about enemy bombardment. Many of those who remained would have had to part from family members, through evacuation or because of service in the armed forces. Some would have experienced bomb damage at close hand (occasionally from British anti-aircraft shells), or, when ordnance fell unexploded, would have had to leave their homes until the bomb or shell was found and made safe (Denford, 2008).

The effect on the Trust's work

No more houses were acquired by the Trust during the War; instead it turned its attention to keeping its homes habitable, employing a direct labour team of six to ensure as quick a response as possible to the damage caused.

> *'During the worst of this period we had to go round our properties every day to see if all was well. The fifty houses were very scattered so this was no easy task…we found all the inhabitants of one of the houses wandering in the road; they had been bombed out. Fortunately some tenants of another house had been evacuated, so there were a certain number of vacant rooms and we had to make what use we could of these.'* (Hill, 1961)

These years saw many more changes of tenancy among the Trust's tenants then hitherto. In the first year of the war, 60 tenancies changed hands, out of just over 240: many tenants were evacuated, and others moved out of London away from danger. There was no shortage of new applicants for any vacancies:

> *'The demand for accommodation of all sorts is insatiable, especially in view of the large number of people who have come from the more heavily bombed districts in the South and East of London'* (AGM1 1942)

The TAF minutes refer to new tenants arriving who had been evacuated – or evacuated themselves – from Dover; from Plymouth, and even refugees from Belgium. There is discussion at one meeting about whether the whole Committee of Management should be involved in tenant selection; but in the end it was agreed to leave this to Margaret Hill and Norah Clegg.

HOUSES DAMAGED IN AN AIR RAID on 21st March, 1944:-

      47 Cecile Park
      72 " "
      74 " "
      76 " "

      90 Crouch Hill.

      33, Lynmouth Road.

<u>47 Cecile Park</u>, 2 places in roof where incendiaries came through, broken mantel piece, hole in floor. (The two men were at home so were able to put out fire while the women fetched water for them - otherwise it could easily have been as bad as the other houses.)

<u>72 Cecile Park</u>, Mrs. Hughes and Mr. Wolfe were the heroes who put out the fires. Miss Hester's bed and bedding were destroyed and the Town Hall sent replacements to her.

<u>74 Cecile Park</u>, Topfloor burnt right out.
Miss Stewart and Mrs. Wood, Town Hall billeted them.
Mrs. Jessers was taken to the Gate Home.
Mrs. White went to her son.
Miss Simmons was taken to the Gate Home.
Miss Bell " " " Bishopswood Home.
Miss Staples went to relatives.

<u>76 Cecile Park</u>, Mrs. Pellatt had a narrow escape - a bomb fell on to her bed, which she had just left, and broke the bed but did not explode. She was taken to Bishopswood Home.

<u>90 Crouch Hill</u>. Windows broken, and an outer door displaced. All tenants were able to remain there.

<u>33, Lynmouth Road</u> had a 4' 6" Rocket Shell case through roof into attic.

The Hornsey Gas Company have taken the meters from No. 74 Cecile Park. They promise not to use them elsewhere but hold them for us, to be put back when house is repaired. This we believe the Council will do quickly.

The Hornsey Electricity Company will decide whether or not they will take the meters away, but if they do, they will definitely put them back for our tenants when the house is repaired.

A report of bomb damage to Trust properties from an air raid on 21st March 1944, pasted in to the hand-written Committee of Management minute book.
London Metropolitan Archives, City of London ACC/1523/003

One persistent issue discussed at the Committee of Management was how to repair the war damage to the Trust's houses. Where a house was owned leasehold, the freeholder had to be notified, of course. The Treasurer, Mr Paine, suggested that the Trust should undertake no more 'First Aid Repairs', but leave them to the Council who would not have to be paid until after the war. The problem was the delay that this would cause, the Council having so much work to address. The ingenious solution agreed was to ask the Council to appoint the Trust itself as an approved builder, so it could carry out its own repairs as if it were the Council itself.

Changing role of the Tenants' Assistance Fund
The issues dealt with by the TAF also changed, of necessity; and through the minutes of their meetings, we can get a flavour of life during wartime.

> 'A great deal had happened since the last meeting as so many of the families had been evacuated. Mrs Hill said that the HHT had allowed each tenant a week's rent in the case of their having large families and a lot of things to buy before the evacuation.' (TA1 21/9/39)

> 'It was discussed whether it would be advisable to recommend a reduction in rents to the HHT where husbands and sons were serving with the Forces' (TA1 17/7/40)

New calls on TAF funds arose: 'F is joining up and he and Mrs F wished to see their children who were evacuated to Somerset, so the TAF gave them £2 towards their fares' (TA2 17/9/40). At the same time, the TAF continued to assist as before with home helps, support for elderly tenants, and so on. 'M H has got a good job and Mrs H had to buy her a coat and dress for work. So £3 is to be given her to help her with this.'

(TA2 5/8/42). The minute book shows the Committee continuing to take a close and active interest in the lives of tenants:

> 'Mr F is in the army and is being sent to Palestine for 2 years. Mrs F very upset.' (TA1 10/4/40)

> 'Mrs W goes out to work, and her little girl is very neglected, the committee have asked Mrs Hill to speak to Dr Garrow about her. The house is unspeakably dirty. (TA2 11/3/41)

We do not know how the Trust dealt with tenants who moved away from London for safety reasons but wished to return in the future. It appears that this was tolerated:

> 'Mrs W evacuated to Wales to her mother – her husband is in France – she is expecting another baby. She is badly in arrears, but it is thought she will pay up on her return.' (TA2 8/11/44).

There are several mentions of rooms on the top floors of houses being used to store furniture at a notional rent, presumably because they were least popular as most vulnerable to bomb damage. At the end of 1940, the Committee paid tribute to its tenants:

> 'Fortunately none of the tenants suffered personal injury and they have without exception behaved admirably in most trying and nerve-wracking conditions. Loss of prized and irreplaceable possessions has in no single instance been openly bemoaned and a spirit of helpfulness under difficulty has shown the superficiality of the small and often unreasonable grumbles in ordinary times.'

Throughout the war, the TAF Committee remained largely the same. The rent collectors continued to visit regularly, and there is even mention of a fundraising whist drive and tea at one point (TA 19/11/41). However, the meetings of the Committee diminished in number as the war progressed, from monthly in the 1930s, to seven in 1940, to five in 1941, four in 1942, and three in each of the years 1943/1944/1945. This may in part have been due to the competing calls on Margaret Hill's energy and attention.

Margaret Hill's war

As Chairman of Hornsey Borough Council's Billeting Sub-Committee, Councillor Hill was responsible for accommodating several hundred Belgian refugees, some of whom were once again sheltered in Alexandra Palace. But the job was even bigger than that:

> *'Those resident in the south and east of London were the first victims of the raids…The north of London was considered at that time to be a comparatively safe area, and busloads of people were sent there when their houses were destroyed.'* (Hill 1961).

In addition, housing was sought for some chronic invalids in order to free up hospital beds for military casualties. The Council's strategy was to requisition some large houses in the Borough, left empty by their owners, to provide immediate respite.

While younger people adapted to their changed circumstances readily, older and frailer people needed more support, and there was soon seen to be merit in accommodating them separately from family groups. This was an area where Councillor Hill's experience of setting up the Delia Grotten House was deemed valuable. She mobilised the small committee who supervised that House, and with the approval of the Ministry of Health within a few days had requisitioned two neighbouring houses in Hampstead Lane. Within a week or two they had sourced the furnishings and equipment needed to house thirty-three older people, a matron and two nurses, from friends, neighbours and a raft of organisations including the Canadian and American Red Cross.

Next into view came the Sanatorium of Highgate School – empty since the school had been evacuated, and situated opposite a First Aid Post. Late in 1940, this too was requisitioned and equipped for sixteen residents, with a skeleton staff supplemented by the nurses from the First Aid Post, when their duties allowed. These two establishments, and the three that followed (including the house of the Hills' next door neighbour), were unusual in that they provided a degree of support for their 110 residents as well as housing: most of the emergency hostels elsewhere in London were only for the able-bodied. Thus was the concept developed of a 'halfway house' between hospital and home, on which Margaret Hill's second big project – Hill Homes – was to be built.

And in addition to her Council work, the day to day management of the five requisitioned homes, and chairing the ongoing work of Hornsey Housing Trust, Margaret Hill took on two national roles: as the first Chair of the National Old Persons' Welfare Committee in 1941; and membership of the Nuffield Trust Survey Committee on the Problems of Ageing and the Care of Old People in 1943, chaired by Seebohm Rowntree.

Meanwhile the work of Hornsey Housing Trust carried on. The financial accounts continued to be drawn up, and there are several mentions of the rent income remaining steady, with few vacancies despite the many changes of tenancy, and very low rent arrears: one reason given is the absence of unemployment during wartime. A major legacy of the war for the Trust was the physical damage suffered by its housing stock, and the management and cost of putting that right. This was to be a challenge for the next decade.

Extracts from the TAF Committee Minute-Book 1939-45

'Mr and Mrs E have both been ill and have had to have a home help for 3 weeks…They are to be taken into Delia Grotten's House when it is ready.' (8/3/40)

'Mr B has got a week behind, so it was decided to let him off the 6d he has been paying for furniture each week and to put his 6d to paying off his arrears' (12/6/40)

'Mrs H is a nice new tenant for the top flat, she has evacuated herself from the S Coast and has a niece in Hornsey' (17/7/40)

'Mrs Hill was unfortunately detained at the Town Hall on refugee business' (17/9/40)

'30 Harvey Road…had an incendiary bomb through the roof' (17/9/40)

'Miss K is the new tenant…she was bombed months ago and has lived in shelters ever since' (11/3/41)

'The electric light situation was discussed at some length and various recommendations were made to raise the amount paid by the different tenants taking into consideration their various circumstances' (23/4/41)

'Mrs W has been taken to Enfield she became violent in her senility' (24/9/41)

'It was suggested that each rent collector should economise time by collecting from one tenant in each house only. Where necessary this tenant should be given 1/- per week for his or her trouble.' (28/1/42)

'The Ws are all home again and the eldest boy is now working – the rent which had been reduced is now to be raised to what it was before.' (20/5/42)

'Mrs P is the new tenant...she is a Durham miner's wife and her husband has had a nervous breakdown and is in hospital. They have 6 children and were found in very poor circumstances, quite a lot of furniture was given to them' (20/5/42)

'It was decided to give Mrs S 2/6 a week to help her with her cleaning and washing as she is 80 years old. The Assistance Board is to be asked if they will make her supplementary pension longer for this purpose' (9/6/43)

'Mr H was given £1 out of the funds for looking after the gardens in the Middle Lane house and for buying seeds etc – he does the gardens most beautifully and receives no pay, it is a very nice occupation for him' (24/5/44)

'Mrs Hill read the riot act to Mrs B Miss H and Miss B. It seems to have had an excellent effect.' (8/11/44)

Transcribed from the hand-written TAF Committee minute book, with minor amendments to protect privacy.

The post-war decade: 1945–1955

The intense six-year period of Hornsey Housing Trust's initial growth, and the huge war-time disruption of the following six years, were followed by a decade of making good in a changed world. There were three main elements to this: bringing its housing stock into good repair; adding to the stock; and supporting its tenants. To help with all this, one of the first actions of the Committee of Management after the war was to employ a professional housing manager, Miss Robertson. It had always been intended that an appointment should be made once the Trust reached a certain size, as it would be unrealistic to expect volunteers to continue with this work indefinitely, but the war had intervened. The sources we have for this decade include the minute book of the main Committee of Management; the records of the AGMs, in some cases supplemented by a Chairman's report; and the minutes of the Tenants' Assistance Fund Committee, which continued to meet till 1956.

Repairing and maintaining the housing stock
The immediate, pressing need was to repair the war damage to the Trust's housing stock. There was some government help for this, but builders and building materials were inevitably in short supply, and in these post-war years housing trusts were not allowed to increase their rents to help pay for repairs and maintenance. Funding was made available by the government from 1941 to repair buildings subject to war damage, and War Damage Claims were still being discussed by the Committee of Management and secured by the Trust up to 1953. Throughout this period the asset value of the stock presented in the annual Accounts stayed the same; but it was accompanied by the note *'Certain houses have been severely damaged by enemy action'* from 1940 through to 1955: we can presume that the war damage had been made good by then.

Government assistance was of necessity supplemented by the Trust's own reserves, built up in the early years, which now needed to be spent on repairs rather than the purchase of new stock. Of course, not all the houses were capable of repair: the site of 95 Mountview Road (which had been destroyed by blast) was sold to Hornsey Borough Council; and 2 Nelson Road was judged incapable of repair, and sold for development. Side by side with this repair work, the usual maintenance cycle was re-established, with 29 of the Trust's houses painted externally in 1948 and 1949; and frequent mentions in the Committee minutes of a programme to maintain the common areas of the houses, especially replacing carpet and linoleum on the stairs.

Through the early 1950s, the minutes also record increasing numbers of issues around management of the electricity supply. It was not always possible to separate out supplies to different tenants, as so many of the flats were not self-contained; the apportioning of costs between several households could then be tricky. By 1955, there were only ten houses left where the Trust itself paid the electricity bill and recharged the tenants.

New properties

One reason for building up reserves – now depleted – had been to expand the Trust's activities into new building. A plot of land in Muswell Hill had been identified during the war, and bungalows designed for it. But by the end of the war, undertaking the development was no longer a realistic option, on financial grounds. The Trust handed over its plans to Hornsey Borough Council, and a small estate was built there, which remains to this day. Respecting the initiative taken by the Trust, the estate was named 'Keynes Close', and a set of iron gates in honour of John Maynard Keynes (paid for by his parents) was erected there.

Drawing of the flats to be named 'Goldsmiths' Court', from the Chairman's Report to the 1949 AGM of Hornsey Housing Trust

Goldsmiths' Court

Meanwhile, Margaret Hill's attention had turned to a site close to Highgate Underground Station. A block of flats there – Coleridge Buildings – had been destroyed by a V2 rocket in 1944. She arranged for the National Corporation for the Care of the Old (on one of whose committees she sat) to secure ownership of the site, and then came to an agreement with the Goldsmiths' Company – one of the city livery companies – to purchase it and pay for the construction of 16 flats there. The plan was for this to be leased to Hornsey Housing Trust in exchange for rehousing some tenants nominated by them; and the Clerk of the Goldsmiths' Company joined the Trust's Committee of Management. Building work started in the summer of 1949, and the opening ceremony took place on 7 September 1950, presided over by the Prime Warden of the Goldsmiths' Company. The Trust had received over 100 applications for tenancies there.

In the minutes of the Committee meetings, there are a number of references during this decade to other properties which the

Trust considered acquiring, but the only purchases completed were 8 Hatherley Gardens in 1951, and 26 Priory Road in 1954. 8 Hatherley Gardens was bought to serve as an office base for the Trust, to be shared with the Hornsey Welfare Committee for Old People formed in 1948 (and chaired by Margaret Hill), with flats above: only a convenient few minutes' walk from Hornsey Town Hall. For 26 Priory Road, there was a discussion about how it might be converted: those familiar with the traditional late Victorian house type can visualise what was planned:

> 'Mr Hendry advised converting the house into 4 separate units as follows (1) the ground floor to consist of 3 separate rooms and a small kitchen and separate bathroom (2) the 1st floor front room and small room (3) 1st floor back and 1st floor back addition (4) 2nd floor front and 2nd floor back. No.s 2, 3 and 4 to share the bathroom on the 1st floor.'

A bathroom shared by three households was still the norm.

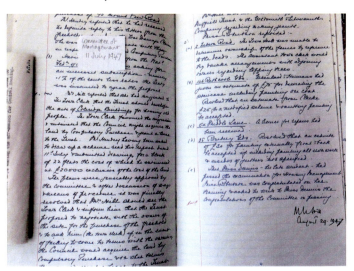

Extract from the minutes of the meeting of the Committee of Management on 11 July 1947. London Metropolitan Archives, City of London ACC/1523/003

Support for the Trust's tenants

With the appointment of Miss Robertson as Housing Manager in 1945, the role of the Tenants' Assistance Fund began to change. Committee meetings, though intermittent, continue to demonstrate a high degree of familiarity with tenants' circumstances: it may be that some of the TAF Committee members continued to collect the rent, or that relationships built up with tenants over the years of rent collection persisted. Norah Clegg's enjoyably frank minute taking continued:

> 'The various tenants were discussed – all seemed to be getting on all right with the exception of Miss B, who was probably leaving, which would be a very good thing' (TA2 10/12/45).

Early in 1946 Miss Robertson took over the role of Secretary from Norah Clegg, and the minutes become rather less lively, but still illuminating about the range of issues the Committee considered:

> 'a large consignment of clothing had come from the Canadian Red Cross and a list was made of those tenants who were most in need. This list is to be sent to Mrs Hill for final decision according to clothing available.'

> 'the question of helping Miss S to get a set of teeth was discussed'

> 'The Ws to be asked to try to make less noise with band practice and to remove motor cycle from front garden.' (TA2 26/11/46)

Increasingly, however, the minutes show examination of individual tenants' needs rather than more general issues arising at specific addresses. Discussion was informed by the co-option on to the Committee, of the Secretary of the Hornsey Welfare Committee for Old People, and at the 12/1/48 meeting, the needs of all of the Trust's tenants who were over 80 years old – 19 of them – were reviewed. One issue that persists through this decade is what to do about older tenants who through mental or physical frailty need additional support, and how this might be provided, for example *'to help tenants who cannot wash their hair and keep themselves clean'* (TA2 20/3/48). The Red Cross provided a weekly service for 2/-; should the TAF sometimes pay for this? The idea of employing someone to help tenants at times of ill health, in exchange for a rent-free flat, was floated.

The minutes record one meeting only in 1952 and then in 1953, followed by a final, brief meeting in 1956. There is no discussion about the ending of the TAF Committee meetings, either in the minute book or at the Committee of Management meetings at that time. It may be that the provision of alternative support following the introduction of the Welfare State had made its function redundant. As Margaret Hill said in her 1949 Chairman's Report:

> *'now there are available for the infirm, Home Helps, Meals-on-Wheels for those who cannot get out to shop; also ... visitors from Hornsey Old People's Welfare Committee give a great amount of voluntary help and advice on difficulties of every kind. All this in addition to the amenities supplied by the National Assistance Board officers. Such excellent assistance would have shaken the old 'Guardians' to the core!'*

The 124th Meeting of the Committee held at 16 Bishopswood Road

Thursday 24th April 1952 at 11 AM
Present: Mrs Hill Chairman, Mrs Clegg, Mrs Hendry, Miss Alexandra, Miss Pass, Messrs Hendry, Prideaux and Paine. Miss Goldsmith also attended.

1. **Minutes of last Meeting** and Special Meeting were read and confirmed.
2. **Matters arising:**
    (a) 62 Denton Road: resolved to supply a geyser for the bath subject to Miss Goldsmith being able to arrange with the 4 tenants to pay 6d each per week towards the cost estimated at £31.
    (b) 70 Rathcoole Gardens: The Secretary reported completion of the purchase of the ground rent of £7 for £200, and request to Messrs Kenneth Brown to hold the deeds for safe custody
    (c) 8 Hatherley Gardens: The Secretary reported completion of Messrs Hollings contract for repairs and alterations and payment of their account £612-12-5 and architects fees £63 and read letter of thanks to Mr Hendry for his services and modified charge.
    (d) 2 Nelson Road: read letters to agents asking them to find a purchaser at £650 or near offer. The Secretary was instructed to accept an offer of £450 received through Messrs Norman if unable to get it increased to £500.

3. **Secretary's report:**
    (a) Balance at bank 31 March 1952 £702-14-8.
    (b) Read letter to Bank Manager asking him to arrange for Miss Goldsmith to have facilities for use of Night Safe similar to those accorded to Miss Robertson.
    (c) Read letter from National Federation of Housing Societies,

regarding financial provision for repairs and draft reply thereto which was approved

(d) *Read letter to Miss Robertson regretting her resignation and cause thereof through serious illness*

(e) *Reported further donation of £17-14-0 from DS and read letter of thanks*

(f) *Reported registration of Probate of Mrs R and read a letter from Mr R expressing willingness to take up £100 loan stock if the Trust required money. The Committee instructed the Secretary to accept the offer and send form of application to Mr R.*

4. *Submitted the **Auditors' report and accounts** for the year ended 31 December 1951. Resolved that these be approved and submitted to the General Meeting to be called for Thursday 29 May. Auditors' request for a modest increase of fee by five guineas was unanimously agreed and thanks expressed for their services.*

5. **Miss Goldsmith reported**: *Goldsmith's Court: She considered the quantity of fuel was very large and on investigation found that the heating of the flats was excessive. She had arranged for the heat to be turned on later in the morning and turned off earlier at night, and thereby hoped that considerable economy would result. The Committee expressed their approval and appreciation. She also suggested on the advice of the engineer that a maintenance contract for the boiler should be entered into. Mr Hendry was asked to arrange terms with the engineers.*

Flat tenants complained of disturbance through the constant singing by Miss L-S a professional singer. The Secretary was instructed to write asking that the nuisance be abated.

Minute of a meeting of the Committee of Management, transcribed from the hand-written minute book with minor amendments to protect privacy.

Management of the Trust

There was a good deal of continuity within the management of the Trust through the growth years and the war years, and for the decade after. Of the ten members of the Committee of Management in 1936, seven (of eight) were still there in 1946. Indeed, there were still four of the original members on the Committee in 1956, one of whom (Mr Paine) had acted as Secretary and Treasurer for eighteen years. Nowadays, merit is seen in shorter terms for membership of Boards and Committees – the current National Housing Federation guidance is six years, with extension to nine exceptionally. But given the pace of change in the Trust's first dozen years, continuity will have had value.

Another contrast with today, is that there was no bar on Committee members of a Trust accepting paid work from it. When the 1974 Housing Act introduced public funding for housing associations, it also necessarily outlawed 'dualities of interest' whereby a Committee member could benefit personally from work paid for by the organisation. But before that it was not unusual for a housing trust or association to elect on to its committee someone with a professional background interested in the organisation but also prepared to offer their services in exchange for a fee. A key member of Hornsey Housing Trust's Committee of Management in these post-war years was an architect, Duncan Hendry. Not only did he professionally advise on many matters relevant to the maintenance of the housing stock, he prepared the drawings for Goldsmiths' Court and ran the building contract. There is mention of him being thanked for charging a reduced fee for much of the work he carried out, but no hint of a suggestion that this was in any way untoward, however unusual that may seem to us today. There was continuity also amongst the employed staff. Miss Robertson resigned due to ill health in 1952 and was replaced by her assistant Miss Goldsmith, who retained her post until her retirement in

1970. Len Belfall continued to work for the Trust from 1936 until he retired in 1983.

Margaret Hill's personal involvement was key to the continuity of management at the Trust. From its first meeting in 1933 until 1958, she chaired both the Committee of Management and (until it stopped meeting in 1956) the Tenants' Assistance Fund Committee; and the meetings of both were held in her house, as were the Annual General Meetings. Indeed, the administration of the Trust was from a basement room there until the purchase of 8 Hatherley Gardens. But during this post-war decade the Trust was only one of her commitments. She had set up another Public Utility Company in Hornsey, Hill Homes, in 1944 in order to provide permanent housing for the 110 elderly people for whom she had secured (and managed) accommodation during the war, who needed housing with daily support. For this she needed to fundraise, to buy and convert property, to employ staff and (somewhat inevitably) Chair that organisation too – with Norah Clegg as Secretary. She also set up and chaired Hornsey's own Welfare Committee for Old People, with a familiar mix of volunteer and paid participants, to provide and signpost support for the older people in the borough, funded by Hornsey Borough Council.

Meanwhile, she continued to take on commitments outside Hornsey. Participation in the Nuffield Survey on the Problems of Ageing and the Care of Old People required her to visit housing schemes all over the country, and, she later said, helped her to clarify her own thinking about what worked well. The recommendations of this body led to the establishment of the National Corporation for the Care of Old People in 1947, and she served on its Advisory Council for the next seven years. She gave several lectures in 1951 and 1952 about the care of older people, and was awarded a CBE in 1957 for her services.

Thoughout this time, her support for the Trust was consistent, but there is a suggestion in her later writing that she relished its early, heady days most:

'In 1955 we felt able to expand again and another house was bought and converted into four flatlets. By this time the Housing Trust had changed its character; it had, of necessity to become much more formal. The "red tape" which had hampered us so little before the war now restricted our activities in every direction....The Housing Trust had become of necessity slow, staid and conventional. As a regrettable consequence it had lost its youthful exuberance.' (Hill, 1961)

**Portrait of Margaret Hill, date unknown.
Hornsey Housing Trust Archives**

Consolidation: 1955-1970

By 1955, the primary objective of the Housing Trust had become clear:

'Our policy now is to house as many elderly people as possible and to reduce the number of family units, many of whom are now occupying accommodation which is unsuitable for growing families' (Chairman's report, 1955)

The main sources we have for the next fifteen years are the minutes of the Committee of Management, and the AGM minutes, which usually included a Chairman's report on the activities of the preceding year. The Tenants' Assistance Fund continued to exist, fuelled by interest on donations, and was utilised on occasion by the Committee (for instance, to help with tenants' heating costs in the winter), but there are no lively minutes to provide an insight into housing management issues and tenants' lives. And the unpublished biography of Margaret Hill largely moves on to her work with Hill Homes and family life.

    The Committee of Management generally met four to six times a year over this period (though unusually in 1955 and 1956 it only met twice). The explicit policy of the Trust during this period was *'consolidation, not expansion'* a phrase which first appears in the minutes of a 1959 Committee meeting, and is repeated subsequently. There are two main pieces of evidence which bear this out. The first is that the Committee's attention was largely taken up with the bread-and-butter issues related to the running of the organisation – in particular, the condition of its housing stock, and matters relating to its tenants. The second is that the financial climate was not conducive to expansion: the Trust couldn't afford it.

The bread-and-butter issues

There was plenty to do to keep the existing stock in good repair. By the 1960s, many of the houses owned by the Trust were twice the age they were when first acquired, and needed attention to keep them windproof and watertight. Rain-water goods needed replacing, damp proof courses had failed; and the owners of neighbouring houses complained about trees needing cutting back, or fences rotting. Inside, the common parts were subject to constant wear and tear from the several households sharing access to their rooms. Even at Goldsmiths' Court, the main boiler needed replacing only thirteen years after installation. Meanwhile the expectations of tenants were rising, in line with those of the general population. Hot water geysers over baths were requested, and then electric heaters in bathrooms. Tenants in a newly converted house asked for a telephone line.

Tenancy related issues made their way on to the Committee agenda from time to time – presumably when Miss Goldsmith, who managed all the tenancies with (mostly) only part-time assistance, considered that a matter needed a Committee-level decision. What to do about a tenant who had sublet a room and taken in a lodger? Could she let a flat with steep stairs to a young couple rather than an elderly person? The range of her responsibilities is impressive, not least in dealing with the waiting list – 2,000 applications were received in 1957 alone. At one point, there was discussion about setting up a sub-committee to deal with the selection of new tenants; but the minutes record:

> *'As most of the Trust's accommodation was not self-contained it should be left to the Housing Manager to decide in view of her knowledge of the existing tenants in the house.' (CM1 17/10/60)*

Given the shared facilities in most of the Trust's houses, selecting new tenants able to get on with existing residents would have been very desirable.

A useful snapshot of the ages of the Trust's older tenants is included in the 1957 Chairman's Report:

'212 of our tenants are Old Age Pensioners. Of these 4 are over 90 years of age, 31 over 80 and 102 over 70. 16 of these tenants have been with us for over 20 years and one for 24 years, that is since 1933, the year the Trust started.

It is a striking fact that throughout the 24 years of the existence of the Trust, some 90% of the old people have remained until the end in their own homes, very few having died in hospitals or institutions. This shows how important it is to provide small, easily run flatlets for old people, for if small and convenient enough, they are able and like to run them themselves, and to remain in their own homes all their lives.'

Over this period there were several changes in Committee membership, with the departure of several long-standing members who had been part of the early days of 'youthful exuberance.' Margaret Hill stepped down from the Chair in 1958, aged 73, the year after receiving her CBE. Mr Paine retired the same year as Margaret Hill, after 18 years as Secretary and Treasurer. And five years later, Mr and Mrs Hendry decided to move out of London and left the Committee. Successor Committee members were found, of course. Margaret Hill herself had introduced the man who was to succeed her as Chairman, the Rev Leslie Stringer; and she also made sure the links with Hornsey Borough Council remained strong by bringing in Councillor Hugh Rossi, soon to be Chairman of the Housing Committee. She retired from the Committee of Management in 1959, and in 1961 published her only book, *An Approach to Old Age and its Problems*, distilling what she had learned from her work with older people.

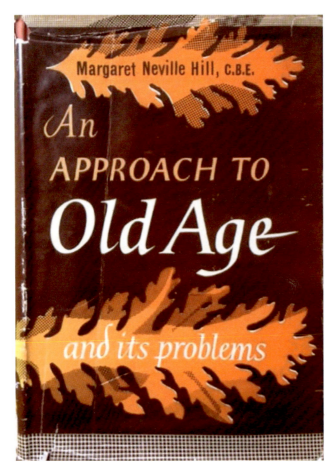

Front cover of 'An Approach to Old Age and its problems', Margaret Hill, 1961

Balancing the books

It needs to be remembered that at this time Hornsey Housing Trust operated largely without public subsidy. It received private subsidy, of course – loan stock investment from those willing to forego some interest in a good cause. And it benefitted from the low interest rates charged by the Public Works Loan Board and passed on by Hornsey Borough Council for the loans it provided. But it still needed to balance its books each year by deciding how much rent to charge and how much to spend. Up until the Housing Repairs and Rents Act 1954 it was not permitted to increase rents, which for some tenants had meant twenty years without a rent increase. That legislation provided some latitude for rent increases where the proceeds were to be spent to improve the condition of the housing stock. Rents were raised by two pence in a shilling in 1954, increasing the rent roll from £7,500 to £9,700. From then on, the issue of whether to increase the rent, and how the increase should be determined, recurs on the Committee agendas, together with the consequential budget for spending on repairs and maintenance.

In 1956 came discussion of a possible policy of *'differential rents'*, that is charging better off tenants higher rents. There was *'concern at the number of families in receipt of high wages who were occupying flats at very low rents'* (CM1 2/8/56). Miss Goldsmith was asked to explore how many tenant households included adult children who were themselves in employment and could contribute more to the rent. Margaret Hill was supportive of this idea, which Hornsey Borough Council itself adopted in due course. However, it was eventually decided not to take the matter further – a rare example of the Chairman (as she still was) not achieving her aim; though the issue did not entirely go away, reappearing for discussion in 1963 under the guise of charging lower rents to poorer tenants.

While the Trust tussled with the problems of the rising costs of materials and labour, and rent levels, it nevertheless continued to pursue a policy of converting the leasehold ownership of its homes to freehold when possible – and affordable. Much of the housing stock it had bought in the 1930s was purchased leasehold. This was not unusual at the time: freehold ownership was often vested in corporate bodies who benefitted from the annual ground rents, and an appreciating asset as a lease neared its end. However, as the years progressed and the length of the leases declined, it was clearly in the interests of the Trust to purchase the freehold interest where possible. And it seems often to have found a willing seller: the post war decades saw a precipitous fall in the size of the private rented sector – from 53% of all housing in the UK in 1950, to 20% in 1970 – and investment in freeholds of ageing properties may no longer have seemed attractive. The Chairman's report of 1957 says that half the houses were now owned freehold, half leasehold. And the Committee minutes record a persistent push to buy more; as an example, at its meeting on 9/11/67 the Trust agreed terms to buy five freeholds (242 Ferme Park Road, 33 Lynmouth Road, 80, 84 and 117 Rathcoole Gardens) and to enquire into the purchase of the freeholds of 110, 112 and 116 Hillfield Avenue. Securing ownership of the freeholds, like investment in the stock, was entirely consistent with the policy of consolidation.

Buying, selling and new building

That said, it would be wrong to conclude that *'consolidation not expansion'* meant no activity by the Trust in buying and selling properties, or even in new building. At many of its meetings over these fifteen years, the Trust considered new purchases – how many tenancies could be accommodated, what rents might be charged, whether the Council's District Valuer would approve the price and the Council might fund the purchase. And occasionally, houses were bought: 94 Crouch Hill in 1959, for example, and 5 Hatherley Gardens in 1969. Also, over the same period, some houses were sold. 10 Pembroke Road – the Trust's first purchase – was the subject of a Council Compulsory Purchase Order as part of its Campsbourne clearance and new building project. 80 Rathcoole Gardens was sold in 1970 due to its poor condition, and 39 Burgoyne Road because of its unsuitability for older tenants, owing to its steep steps.

Over this period, three major projects engaged the Committee, two of which involved acquisitions: the purchase and conversion of 3 Waverley Road; the construction of a block of nine flats in the gardens of 77/79 Middle Lane (which the Trust already owned); and the purchase of 49 Oakfield Road and construction there of Norah Clegg House. All ended up fully let, but none were problem-free.

3 Waverley Road: This was a very large house, bought in 1958 to convert to ten or twelve flatlets. Although Hornsey Council agreed to a loan for the purchase and conversion work, and approved the plans, the project ran into difficulties: the Trust had taken the view that four WCs were adequate to provide for the needs of ten households; but the Ministry of Housing were insisting on two extra WCs. Should the Trust reclassify the house as a 'hostel' (only one bathroom and two WCs required)?; in the end the extra WCs were reluctantly provided, at extra cost. (The Trust also decided to appoint a 'House Mother' to help manage the house: one bonus was that the Ministry would waive the requirement for coal bunkers on each landing.) In letting the flats, three prospective tenants refused on the grounds that they would not have separate kitchens, which suggests that tenant expectations were continuing to rise (the house was demolished in 1983 and the current block of flats built on the site).

Margaret Hill Court: 77 Middle Lane had been bought in 1936, and No.79 in 1938. They were big houses with sizeable grounds, and in the late 1950s the Committee asked Mr Hendry to draw up plans for a block of nine bed-sitting rooms to be built in the back gardens. Negotiations were opened with the Council for a loan, which was conditional on the Trust letting four flatlets to tenants decanted from the Campsbourne clearance area. This was accepted in principle, but led to some to-ing and fro-ing: Miss Goldsmith judged only one of the applicants put forward a '*a possibility*' (two being '*entirely unsatisfactory*'); Mr Rossi asked the Housing Department to find more applicants etc. In the event, all the nominees from the Council turned down offers on account of the small size of the rooms and the level of rent. The flats were all let in 1961 (Margaret Hill Court and Nos 77 and 79 Middle Lane were demolished and Margaret Hill House built on the site in 1992).

Norah Clegg House: The site of 49 Oakfield Road was bought in 1963 from Middlesex County Council: it was a corner site, and Mr Hendry drew up plans for four one bedroomed flatlets, and four two-bedroomed flats. The Trust decided to buy the site with its own funds, but ask Hornsey Council for a loan for the building costs: Mr Rossi was thanked for his work in helping to secure the funding. As the work progressed to tender, and after the tender was let, estimated costs rose, with some consequential calculations about the effect on eventual rent levels. The flats were completed and occupied in 1965, after the granting of some additional subsidies, including Expensive Site Subsidy (further work was undertaken in later years to self-contain all the flats, and to install a lift).

The first two of these schemes seem to have run into difficulties

Norah Clegg House

in letting in respect of the amenities provided – the size of the rooms and the shared facilities – as well as the rents charged. It is worth noting that half the flats in the last – Norah Clegg House – were built as self-contained, with their own bathrooms and kitchens; and that around the same time, the Committee expressed the desirability of incorporating more amenities into existing houses when vacancies arose, that is, moving towards self-containment. So far as the rent levels are concerned, it seems to have been the shared understanding of the Committee that each scheme should be funded independently: that is, the rents on each scheme needed to pay for the cost of providing that scheme. So disquiet about increasing cost estimates is sometimes followed in the minutes by discussion about consequential rent levels, and the need for these to be approved by Hornsey Council. There is no explicit discussion about the idea of pooling rent income across the Trust to pay for new housing, apart from a revealing minute in 1962 that *'it was decided that it would be unwise to increase the rents of existing tenants to provide accommodation for future tenants in view of the ever-mounting cost of labour and materials.'* (CM1 7/6/62)

The *'consolidation, not expansion'* policy seems to have been the right one at the time. In 1963 this was further underlined in the Committee minutes by the Rev Stringer:

> 'The Chairman expressed the view that the cost of land and the cost of building would make it increasingly difficult for Societies and Trusts such as ours to expand since we could not fix rents which would meet the needs of the aged and the poor for whom the Trust was founded' (CM1 19/5/63)

And so it was agreed early the following year:

> 'in the immediate future any expansion of the Trust should be suspended owing to high costs' (CM1 31/1/64)

Departures and new beginnings

There is evidence during these years of the continuing close relationship between the Trust and Hornsey Borough Council, reinforced by the presence of several Hornsey Councillors on the Committee, including Margaret Hill herself and Norah Clegg, Olive Anderson (one time Mayor of Hornsey), and in the latter years Councillor Hugh Rossi. In 1958, the Council asked the Trust if they could do more to help with the Borough's housing problems – including rehousing tenants still occupying requisitioned houses, 13 years after the end of the war. This relationship would of necessity have changed in 1965 with the amalgamation of Hornsey, Wood Green and Tottenham Councils to form the new Borough of Haringey; but the new Borough continued to support the Trust substantially in the following decade.

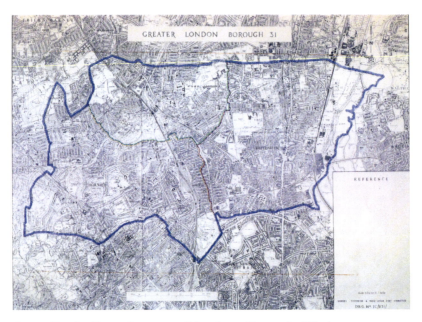

Greater London Borough map 31, of the planned borough of Haringey comprising the existing boroughs of Hornsey, Wood Green and Tottenham, 1965, with minor addition to enhance clarity. By permission of Bruce Castle Museum (Haringey Archive and Museum Service).

(Hugh Rossi went on to win the parliamentary seat of Hornsey in 1966 but stayed on the Committee of Management until 1979 – though he could rarely attend meetings, he would have been a useful ally.)

There are a number of ways in which the years around 1970 mark a time of change for the Trust. Some changes were departures: Margaret Hill 'President and Founder' died in 1970, aged 85; though she had left the Committee of Management a decade before, she remained closely connected to the Trust, indeed the Annual General Meetings had continued to be held in her house until 1966. Miss Goldsmith retired as Housing Manager after eighteen years in post, in the same year. The Chairman, Rev Stringer, retired from the Trust in 1972; and then Norah Clegg died in 1973, still a Committee member; and Mr Prideaux, the Goldsmith's Company representative, retired in 1974 after 24 years. Other changes marked new starts: a new Housing Manager, and new Committee members. In 1971, for the first time, the Trust was working within a borough where the Labour Party had political control. And on the horizon was new legislation introducing public subsidy for housing associations, which would provide new opportunities for the Trust.

Modernisation : 1970-1985

In this next phase of the Trust's development, at first little changed. Issues with the day-to-day repairs and cyclical maintenance programmes surface in the minutes: more fire precaution work was needed; chimney stacks needed repointing; new doorbells were needed at Norah Clegg House. Could the Trust afford to install pay telephones at the houses where no tenant owned a phone, for use in emergency? The issue of the Archway Road widening scheme, and the effect on Goldsmiths' Court, threads its way through the Committee minutes. The purchase of remaining freeholds continued, including a long-winded negotiation with the David and Mary Greig Trust who owned the freeholds of four houses in Hillfield Avenue, eventually resolved by giving them one house back in exchange for the freeholds of the remaining three.

At the 1972 AGM, the new Chairman, Mrs Hetherington, *'referred to the fact that a great deal of improvement was still needed to many properties, in particular in increasing the number of bathrooms'*. And the next year *'she expressed her regret that so little work of improvement to properties had been possible but hoped that some would be started soon'*. The Trust was caught between the need for extra investment in the stock, and the need to keep the rents at an affordable level when the price of building materials and labour was rising. Meanwhile the pressure was on from the Council and from government to raise living standards in the housing stock. The Trust doubled its expenditure on improvements in 1973 compared to 1971, and *'they had all been worthwhile improvements, but had resulted in very few self-contained flats.'* (CM1 10/12/73).

There is an interesting snapshot of the amenities within the Trust's housing stock in 1975, which forms part of the Chairman's Review referred to below. Only 46 of its 258 tenancies were of self-contained flats at that point with their own bathroom and kitchen (16 of them at Goldsmith's Court). Meanwhile, at the other extreme, six or seven households were still sharing one bathroom and two WCs in some houses in Cecile Park and Hillfield Avenue. There was a lot of work to be done.

Fair rents

By then, however, the first of two key pieces of legislation had been enacted which would change the outlook for the Trust. The first was the introduction of 'fair rents' for council and housing association tenants in the Housing Finance Act 1972, together with rent rebates (for council tenants) and rent allowances (for housing association tenants). The Government's intention was that all rents should rise, but poorer tenants should receive a rebate or allowance. This would have a similar outcome to the 'differential rents' scheme introduced by Hornsey Borough Council, and discussed but not adopted by Hornsey Housing Trust; but both the rent setting and the criteria for – and level of – rebate or allowance would be taken out of the hands of the landlord. Either landlord or tenant could apply to have a fair rent registered for a tenancy, but this had to be approved by a local rent officer, on the basis that it ignored both personal circumstances and scarcity.

Councils objected strongly to the system, which removed their right to set their own rents, and were taken out of the scheme three years later, but housing associations stayed within the fair rent regime until 1989. The Trust, like other housing associations, was encouraged to register all its rents, and it decided to introduce them in September 1973, side by side with the new rent allowance scheme. The immediate outcome was an increase in its overall income from rent, up from £528 to £688 per week, while the bill for rent allowances was paid by government. This was welcome, but not going to be a game-changer.

That came the following year with the second piece of legislation, the Housing Act 1974, which introduced a new financing system for housing associations. The new subsidies would enable the Trust to engage in a large programme of investment, and to convert almost all of its older housing into the self-contained accommodation which tenants now sought, and government wished to encourage. It is interesting, reading the minutes of Committee meetings at that time, how little this seems to have been anticipated: the new arrangements clearly took some time to bed in. Indeed, the Chairman Mrs Hetherington produced a personal *Review of the Trust* in April 1975 which for the first time broaches the topic of the Trust amalgamating with another housing association, as a way forward:

Front page of the Housing Act 1974

> 'Over a period of years the Trust will have to meet the current requirements for self-contained units but the nature of many of the Trust's properties is such that this requirement could only be met by converting some properties into family units, so reducing the total number of lettings. This would result in a reduction of lettings for old people and thus, to a large extent, a change in the Trust's present policy....

> ...Implementation by the Trust may be slow because of the difficulty (already experienced) of purchasing new properties for decanting purposes. The large amount of work involved will make it necessary to strengthen the Committee of Management and also the Trust's staff to assist the Housing Manager.
>
> Implementation might, for a number of reasons, be facilitated by amalgamation with another Association....joining with another relatively small Association operating locally or with a large national Association.' (CM2 14/4/75)

The Review was discussed, and it was agreed to explore the issues further. It was reported subsequently that the Deputy Borough Valuer had *'expressed surprise'* that the Trust might amalgamate with another housing association – the borough didn't seem to share the Trust's pessimism; indeed, a meeting with the current Mayor resulted in an invitation to her to join the Committee. There is no further mention of amalgamation. But by then, the Trust's first application for Housing Association Grant had been submitted.

Housing Association Grant (HAG), and Revenue Deficit Grant (RDG)

The Housing Act 1974 provisions were intended to galvanize housing association activity in the UK, and they did. While councils had taken on the heavy lifting of slum clearance and new building after the Second World War, there was seen to be a 'complementary and supplementary' role for housing associations to perform, in particular buying and improving individual houses in the existing mainly Victorian stock – especially in the newly designated Housing Action Areas and General Improvement Areas where there were clusters of homes in poor condition, but not enough to warrant clearance. Housing associations were thought to be smaller, more local, more agile, and perhaps more sensitive managers than councils (though the term 'housing association' covered many different kinds of organisation).

Housing Association Grant, or HAG, was a remarkably generous capital subsidy. The starting point for its calculation was the fair rent which the housing association expected to receive once the dwelling was refurbished. From the rent they could keep prescribed allowances to pay for the cost of management and maintenance and occasional voids; and they then calculated the size of the loan that the remainder could repay: the rest was eligible for HAG. This meant that HAG routinely covered 75–85% of the capital cost of a project – it could even cover 100% if the rent set was exceptionally low. Of course there were controls over the cost, and the standard of the works, purchase prices etc, but the availability of grant subsidy stimulated the activity of many housing associations in local areas, some of which are still with us today – Notting Hill Housing Trust and Paddington Churches HA, for instance (now Notting Hill Genesis), Circle 33 (now Clarion) and so on. And it worked – the housing association sector in England doubled in size between 1976 and 1991.

Revenue Deficit Grant (RDG), introduced at the same time, was a recognition that some housing associations, now no longer in control of the rents they could charge or some of the costs of their work, might fall into deficit; it was a discretionary grant, paid in arrears. In future years, as rents rose, there would be a need to claw back some of the subsidy paid under this legislation; but for the time being, housing associations like the Trust could engage in much more ambitious programmes of work than they had undertaken hitherto.

With this new access to public money, came the requirement for housing associations to be able to demonstrate their probity, by registering with the Housing Corporation – a government quango, set up in 1964 but now with considerably enhanced powers and responsibilities. Registration meant abiding by codes of practice and rules of behaviour – including Committee members not being allowed to profit from the activity of the organisation. Then, as now, the term 'housing association' covered a myriad of different types of organisation: big housing trusts; local voluntary organisations; housing co-operatives and co-ownerships; even some almshouses. All were required to conform to similar standards if they wanted access to the subsidies. Hornsey Housing Trust became a registered housing association in October 1975, and a month later submitted its first HAG application.

Conversion to self-contained flats

From this point, the Committee minutes start to incorporate more and more detail about the improvement and conversion projects in

Street property, Cecile Park N8

prospect. There was planning where to work first; considering plans and drawings; deciding what if any maintenance work needed doing at the same time; acquiring one or two additional dwellings to be used as decants for tenants moving temporarily. Does the Council policy that only a third of properties in each scheme might be bedsitters, apply when housing older people? Should 72/74/76 Cecile Park be converted all together, like 123/125/127 Ferme Park Road? Then there was managing the process of selecting contractors, putting work out to tender, and monitoring progress. There was the need to negotiate HAG rates with the Department of the Environment, particularly when a special case had to be made for excess costs to be funded. Discussions had to be held with Haringey Council about planning issues; meetings with the Borough Valuer are referred to. What about funding? Should the Trust look to the Council or the Housing Corporation for short term loans to cover the works periods? Negotiations were held with the Council about their entitlement to nominations to the completed dwellings.

It must have been gratifying to be able to move forward so swiftly at last. The Chairman's report for the 1976 AGM notes that '*the progress of the Trust in acquiring new properties, and upgrading existing ones, was beginning to show results, and was most encouraging.*' But as she had identified the year before, there was a need for both the Committee and staff to move up a gear. The Committee actively looked for additional Committee members to reinforce the Board. The pressure on the Housing Manager would have increased also: to the usual round of rent collection and tenancy issues was added the need to decant houses in advance of the works programme, moving often elderly tenants either temporarily or permanently into alternative accommodation. One tenant in particular – Mr N of Harvey Road – surfaces more than once in the Committee minutes, determined not to move, though the only remaining tenant in the house. A member of the Borough Valuer's department offered to visit to propose alternative Council accommodation all over the borough (3/4/78); the next month, Mr N was offered a two bedroom maisonette in Ferme Park Road '*He was very impressed by it, but refused because the kitchen was not big enough for all his kitchen furniture*'. Six months later, he refused a flat with a large kitchen in Hillfield Avenue. A year after that, the Committee reluctantly considered legal action to move him.

The scale of the disruption caused by the works was significant. Early in 1977, there were 19 vacant tenancies in properties awaiting works; by late 1978 this figure was 56 (with consequential rent loss which had to be accommodated in the annual budget). Then in 1978, shortly after the Trust moved offices to 36 Haringey Park, Miss Stewart the Housing Manager stepped down. Her successor only stayed for nine months. This may be one of the reasons why the Chairman described 1979 as '*a traumatic and harassing year*' at the AGM. She went on to say that '*conversion work had been limited… and future development was very much limited by government finance restrictions*'. There had of course been a General Election in 1979, won by the Conservatives; a change of government will have created some new uncertainties about future policy over funding. That said, the lead-in and works times for these conversion projects meant that it would be some time before any turning off of the subsidy tap would have an impact. The extract below from the 28/7/80 minutes bears out the scope of the continuing programme: 26 of the Trust's properties are involved in some way.

Impact on the Trust

This investment of public money in the Trust's housing stock was undoubtedly welcome, and for the last forty years, the Trust's tenants have benefitted from it. But for the Trust as an organisation, it required major changes. There were many new requirements to meet, to be eligible for public funding. It had to conform to prescribed building standards, as well as Council policies about conversions in

Current projects: Active

72 – 6 Cecile Park	Completion expected in October
78 Cecile Park	Agreed to write to the owner, Mrs R, and explain reasons for the delay
80 Cecile Park	Purchase of freehold is proceeding slowly. Council finance for our improvement scheme looks doubtful
9 Church Lane	Awaiting a scheme from Peter Mishcon
30 Harvey Road	Tender came in 50% over the estimate. Negotiations will take place to reduce the figure
116 Hillfield Ave	Waiting for a council decision to approve funding
79 Middle Lane	Work almost completed. The two flats affected are now occupied
16 Park Avenue South	Still trying to buy the freehold
2 and 126 Rathcoole Gardens	The offer from London and Quadrant is expected
5 Rathcoole Gardens	Waiting for a council decision to approve funding
7 Rathcoole Gardens	R I Meyer have now prepared a specification and tenders are due on 8th August
70 Rathcoole Gardens	Tender approval received 25/7/80
84 Rathcoole Gardens	On site 18/7/80
3 Waverley Road	A scheme is expected from Peter Mishcon. The Council's financial commitment must be confirmed.

Complete, awaiting interim HAG, Final HAG

90 Crouch Hill, 117 Ferme Park Road, 123–7 Ferme Park Road, 36 Haringey Park, 2 Hatherley Gardens, 8 Hatherley Gardens, 55 Hillfield Avenue, 33 Lynmouth Road, 48 Rathcoole Gardens, 117 Rathcoole Gardens, 120 Rathcoole Gardens

Transcribed from the minutes of the Committee of Management meeting on 28th July 1980, with minor amendments to protect privacy.

the borough. There were standards of compliance over procedures, such as how schemes were tendered and contractors selected. There was the need to get to grips with the approved Housing Corporation format for setting out accounts – referred to as a major headache at several of the Committee meetings.

The Trust took several steps to get on top of all this: it organised some briefings for Committee members and staff on the detail of subsidy requirements and obligations; and in 1979 it appointed its first Finance Officer, and also set up a Development Sub-Committee to focus on the detail of the schemes in process. Then there was a need to professionalise the internal management of the Trust. The National Federation of Housing Associations published guidance on contracts of employment, sick pay, grievance and disciplinary procedures; staff went on NFHA training courses. There was a good deal of pressure on the new Housing Manager, and from time to time she asked the Committee to note the responsibilities which she just did not have time to discharge.

There were also new uncertainties to tolerate. Keeping properties empty for improvement led to a reduction in rent income, and Committee members had to get used to managing a deficit in their budget. Revenue Deficit Grant was discretionary and paid in arrears – the payment for 1980/81 was received in January 1982. It did not help that the Trust still had a number of unmodernised tenancies, and as housing aspirations rose, some of these were difficult to let *'We cannot find anyone on our waiting list to offer three second-floor unconverted flats to'* (CM2 12/3/81) – they were offered to the Council, who couldn't find anyone either. One small flat at 8 Hatherley Gardens was refused by 11 applicants. In 1983 increasing concern about an unfunded deficit led to a decision to sell a house – 62 Denton Road – in order to balance the books. There were also uncertainties about subsidy finance over the longer term. Although there were many projects in the pipeline, there was a moratorium on new projects in late 1980, and worries were frequently expressed about cuts in the future under the new government.

Meanwhile, relations with Haringey Council seem to have remained good, and the Council remained the main lender for HAG-funded schemes, particularly when the Trust had properties in a declared Housing Action Area, such as Hornsey Vale. Alex Henney, recently Chief Housing Officer for Haringey, joined the Board briefly in 1980, and later that year, a formal nomination agreement was signed between Haringey Council and the Trust. Under this, the Council could nominate up to 50% of tenants for newly converted flats, and 60% of relettings and lets to unconverted dwellings. In exchange, the Council agreed to bid for funding for an additional ten houses for the Trust over the next two years (6/11/80). In 1981, Mrs Hetherington retired from the Trust, and Joyce Butler, who had until 1978 been MP for Wood Green and had close connections to the Council, took over the Chair.

Housing management matters
With so much attention demanded by the development programme, tenancy issues surface rarely in the Committee minutes for these years. Where they do, they tend to be in one of two contexts. The first is the codification and formalisation of relations with tenants, and in this it is consistent with the consolidation of the Trust's growing professionalism. In 1981, a tenant consultation policy was agreed, and shortly after a subcommittee was set up to look at the Tenancy Agreement and Information. The following year, two tenants joined the Committee, and the year after that, a Tenancy Sub-committee is mentioned for the first time. Towards the end of 1983 comes the first minuted discussion of ethnicity and equal opportunities:

'At present all the staff are white as are the great majority of our tenants. After discussion the committee agreed that in future we should include in all job advertisements the fact that the Trust is an equal opportunities

employer, also that we should make positive efforts to reach the ethnic minority groups in the community' (CM2 7/11/83).

The second context is a revisiting of that enduring issue, how to provide the extra support that some tenants need as they grow older and more frail. The 1978 AGM notes the appointment of 'good neighbour housekeepers' in Ferme Park Road and Hatherley Gardens, and also pays tribute to the close relationship which the Trust had with Hill Homes, to which some tenants moved when they could no longer sustain their Trust tenancy. A few years later there is a review of the role of caretakers. The practice at the time was to offer a residential flat to caretakers responsible for maintaining the cleanliness of the communal parts of a group of older houses. Living within that group of houses, the caretakers inevitably took on something of a supportive role: might this be developed into a wider 'good neighbour' scheme?

Then in 1982 the Council brought to the market the site of the old Lower Stationers' School in Weston Park. This seems to have been the prompt for a more far-reaching discussion at the Committee of Management: *'If we decide to widen our provision to include sheltered housing, this could help with moving our tenants on from their existing flats when they can no longer cope entirely on their own'.* (CM2 13/12/82). Thus the ground began to be laid for a significant expansion of the Trust's activities over the next fifteen years, in particular into building sheltered housing – including Abyssinia Court, on the Weston Park site.

Expansion: 1985-2000

Forty years before, Margaret Hill had identified the usefulness of building new housing, because it could be specifically designed to meet the needs of older people. Since then, average life expectancy had increased by eight years for women and seven for men – people were living longer, and living with the disabilities and health needs of age. Some of these people would have been Hornsey Housing Trust tenants, who could perhaps no longer manage the stairs in a converted Edwardian house, or living entirely independently, and whose housing needs could only be met by moving to a different landlord or a care home. By 1982, as we saw at the end of the last chapter, the Committee of Management were already considering the benefits of the Trust building its own sheltered housing to provide independent living in suitably designed property, with a modicum of support. Not only was the Committee ready for this, so it seems were the staff: in Joyce Butler's time as Chairman, *'the Trust progressed from*

Waverley Road, N8

being a very small, largely part time and voluntary staffed organisation to becoming the professionally staffed body it is today' (tribute paid by her successor Pamela Marshall in 1993).

As we shall see, these years were a period of expansion for the Trust, in a number of directions. In bald numbers, the Trust built 132 new flats during this period. Some were for tenants with traditional housing needs: 15 flats were finally built on the site of 3, Waverley Road, for example; and a 'design and build' scheme of 13 flats was completed in Pembroke Road, (called Stowell House after one of the original team of rent collectors). But the Trust also expanded the range of older people whose housing needs it aimed to meet. It provided sheltered housing with resident wardens for those who needed extra support. It sought actively to meet the housing needs of older people from minority ethnic groups. And it looked to meet the needs of other people too, building housing designed for young people needing support for their mental health, requiring specialist management. Lastly it expanded where it worked, extending its presence well beyond Hornsey to all parts of the London Borough of Haringey – east to Tottenham, and south to Harringay.

We cannot trace how the decisions were made about the several supported housing schemes which were built in the 1990s, as the minutes of the Committee of Management during this period seem to have been inadvertently lost in the mid-2000s. We do, however, have some other documents to rely on – press cuttings, journal articles, occasional Chairman's reports – and importantly, we have the contribution through interview of Olexandra Stepaniuk, who was the Director of the Trust for these fifteen years.

Tenant involvement in design

The sheltered housing scheme which was to become **Margaret Hill House** was the first to be built. It would not have been an easy decision to demolish two large houses (77 and 79 Middle Lane) and Margaret

Margaret Hill House, showing frontage on Middle Lane

Hill Court, to create the site. But once that decision had been taken, the process which the Trust used to design the scheme cut new ground. A steering group of tenants and staff was set up; they visited other sheltered schemes, where staff talked to staff and tenants to tenants, to identify the features which worked well. They worked closely with the architect (Wilf Marden, of Marden and Knight), and great attention was paid to detail: what door handles were easiest to grip? Which taps? There would be a meeting room, hairdressing room; a hobbies room and greenhouse, and a private garden for the scheme, with a pond and fountain. There would be windows along internal corridors, to replicate the sense of walking down a street.

The external design of Margaret Hill House also needed to fit the streetscape: it would be a prominent corner building on Middle Lane. The architects decided to make the most of this by accommodating the lift, stairs and seating areas in a corner tower. But however good the design, the actual construction of Margaret Hill House was not

> ## Commendation for housing development
> THE eyecatching sheltered housing development in Middle Lane, Crouch End has been recognised by the Civic Trust as an outstanding building in its 1994 awards.
>
> The development, named Margaret Hill House, has been designed by Muswell Hill architects Marden & Knight for the Hornsey Housing Trust.
>
> The building, with its distinctive corner tower, is full of special facilities for elderly residents.
>
> Not seen by the casual passer-by is the private enclosed garden with pond and water channel, and gently splashing fountain.
>
> Margaret Hill House has twenty-three self-contained flats with Warden support, designed to relate sensitively to the varied but strongly Edwardian architecture of the surrounding streets.

From Muswell Record, August 25 1994

straightforward. When it was mostly built, the building contractor filed for bankruptcy, and the part-completed building was left dark and empty for nearly a year. Difficult discussions were held with LB Haringey, the funders, before it was decided that completing the scheme was probably the cheapest option: there was an economic recession, after all, and money might have been lost selling it as it was. A second contractor was found, and the building was finished, and finally occupied in 1992. In vindication of this decision, Margaret Hill House went on to win a Civic Trust Award – a Commendation – in 1994; and was named her favourite building of the year by the then Chair of the National Federation of Housing Associations.

Housing a mix of ethnic groups

The experience of tenant involvement in design at Margaret Hill House was applied to the next sheltered housing scheme, in Weston Park, which was to become Abyssinia Court. The important extra ingredient here, was that the scheme was explicitly designed to meet the housing needs of older people from a mixture of ethnic groups.

Scheme manager and tenants at Abyssinia Court, from Community Care magazine, 14-20 September 1995

There were demographic reasons for this. The ethnicity of Haringey's residents was becoming more mixed; and first generation migrants who had come to the UK to work after the second World War were now of an age when some needed housing with support. In the housing world, there was a degree of acceptance that people as they aged might prefer to live with people of similar backgrounds, with whom they could share their memories, their food preferences, and sometimes their language, their religion. Some housing associations experimented by building sheltered housing for specific groups – as the Trust went on to do at Olive Tree House.

At Abyssinia Court – a large scheme of 36 flats – the Trust decided that it would be let one third to people of African/Afro-Caribbean heritage; one third Asian heritage; and one third European heritage. It was thought that this should help to prevent loneliness for individual tenants, while promoting mixing between groups in the common areas. As at Margaret Hill House, a steering group was set up, this time drawn from all three heritages, to work with staff to influence the design, and to seek out local community groups who might make use of the communal facilities. The work of the steering group was enhanced by the early appointment of a scheme manager who was strongly supportive of the principles of inclusivity on which the scheme was based.

The site was again a prominent one: it had previously housed the Lower Stationers' School, and there was a lot of interest in the neighbourhood about the use to which it would be put. A connection to the local area was cemented by naming the scheme after a local pub, The Abyssinian, that had been demolished in 1971. Although some aspects of the design of Margaret Hill House were repeated – such as avoiding long corridors – a significant difference was that Abyssinia Court was built to a higher level of care – 'close care' as it was called at the time. Although the flats were self-contained, there was scope for providing communal meals (including three separate kitchen areas for Halal, vegetarian and ordinary cooking), and assisted bathrooms for those who might need them. Indeed, it was assumed that all the tenants would have care needs at some level, beyond the informal support of a resident warden.

The Trust took advantage of the scope offered by this significant site, to incorporate its new offices into the design of the ground floor, and moved there when the scheme was completed. Abyssinia Court was funded by the Housing Corporation – with an extra grant to support the high level of tenant participation in project design. It attracted a fair bit of favourable press attention when it opened in 1995, both local (the Hornsey Journal) and in the national specialist press.

Relations with Haringey Council

The success of Margaret Hill House and Abyssinia Court raised the profile of the Trust in Haringey. Olexandra Stepaniuk describes the relationship between the Trust and the Council during this period as *'brilliant'*: both organisations were in agreement about the housing and other needs of older residents. Moreover, at Abyssinia Court the Council were able to nominate all of the new tenants, from their own transfer and waiting list, as they had previously owned the land. The close relationship with the Council continued with the offer of a site in Wightman Road. Although the location of the site was rather further than desirable from a post office and local shops, it was very well located for the Turkish and Greek Cypriot communities who had populated the area around Green Lanes since the partition of the island in 1974. From the start, it was determined that the scheme would be for both communities, and the steering group set up for it included representatives of both: its name, **Olive Tree House**, emphasised their joint heritage. Warm Mediterranean colours were used in the common areas of the scheme, and its courtyard was planted with herbs, for use by the residents.

It was the encouragement of the Council's Commissioner for Mental Health Services which led to the development of 12 supported flatlets in **West Green Road**, using the argument that younger people with mental health difficulties needed a similar kind of housing provision to that which the Trust was providing at its older persons

Olive Tree House

sheltered schemes. It took a little while to get the scheme under way: there were concerns from local residents about the siting of the scheme in their neighbourhood, and the design itself was eventually the subject of a design competition. It helped that the Trust intended to use a specialist organisation to manage the scheme over the long term, subject to a detailed management agreement.

The last sheltered housing scheme built in this period was **Palm Tree Court**, again on a Council-owned site just off Tottenham High Road. This was intended for older people of African and Afro-Caribbean heritage, to enable them to stay in the area in which so many had lived much of their lives – many with family close by. It was completed in 1999.

Quality of life

The steady sequence of years in which these projects were completed is misleading, as it fails to illustrate how the projects would have overlapped both in their planning and their execution. So while one steering group was being set up, another might be in progress, a third scheme on site and a fourth being let. And that's when all was going to plan: hitches would occur in practice – such as the Palm Tree Court builder (as at Margaret Hill House) going bankrupt during the construction period. It will have helped that throughout this period, the Trust employed a Development Manager to keep track of the various projects and maintain the client role.

Throughout all this, the Trust seems to have retained a focus on how its tenants' quality of life might be maintained and improved. Some decisions were about the buildings themselves. With the newly built housing:

> *'One of the greatest challenges was to counter the loneliness people feel as they grow older...with the provision of not just the usual impersonal lounge areas, but informal seating areas around the*

*building to encourage people to sit and chat to their neighbours'.
(Stepaniuk, Mansell News, 1992).*

Then with the older housing stock, where possible lifts were installed – at Hillfield Avenue, Goldsmiths' Court, and Norah Clegg House, for example – to extend the time tenants could remain in their own homes despite any problems with stairs.

Other initiatives related to the way in which the housing would be lived in. There were several tenants on the Committee of Management, and mention of a group of tenants who met regularly with the housing manager. Local volunteers were sought through the Council newsletter (Haringey People), to help tenants settle into their new homes. How might the common parts of the sheltered schemes be best used with activities both for tenants and for the wider local community? A peripatetic warden was employed to support tenants in street properties.

In a number of places, the Trust during this period described itself as a 'community' housing association and there is evidence of active outreach in the press to try to achieve this:

> **HORNSEY HOUSING TRUST**
> is holding a
> **Garden Party**
> for Tenants at
> 3pm Wednesday 8th September 1993
> to celebrate its Diamond Jubilee and
> The European Year for Older People and
> Solidarity between Generations.
>
> We are reserving a limited number of
> **FREE TICKETS**
> for non-tenants who are senior citizens of Hornsey
>
> If you would like to join us please telephone us on:
> **081-340 6374**
> **Hornsey Housing Trust**
> *More Than Just Housing*

General invitation to Diamond Jubilee Garden Party, 1993. Hornsey Housing Trust archive

*'We want to involve the community in our work and we would be pleased to hear from local people and organisations particularly those from ethnic minority backgrounds who wish to join with the Trust – whether it be on the Committee of Management, as a contractor, or as a tenant'
(Caribbean Times 30/11/93).*

In 1998, to help with this, the Trust developed a series of audio tapes in 10 languages about sheltered housing, for which it was Highly Commended by RNIB and won a NOVA award from the Housing Corporation.

The absence of Committee of Management minutes for this period mean that it is more difficult than in previous years to trace the priorities and debates that would have carried on within the organisation. But the 132 new flats built then are the lasting testimony to the Trust's achievement – for those needing sheltered housing as well as those with general needs; for those needing 'close care' as well as informal help; for younger people needing support as well as older people; for citizens of Harringay and Tottenham as well as Hornsey. The Trust was well placed to enter the new millennium with confidence.

Recent years: 2000-2023

The expansion of the previous fifteen years continued during the early years of the new century. With Andrew Billany as Chief Executive from 2000 to 2007 there was further construction, providing housing with support to a new client group, and there was also a significant expansion of services. In 2002, the Trust built two neighbouring schemes at **Sheba Court** in an area of Tottenham under development by Haringey Council: one was a block of sixteen flats and maisonettes; and the other a residential scheme for ten young adults needing support to live independently, to be intensively managed by Haringey Association for Independent Living. The Trust also purchased six individual flats in Tottenham, on developments built by Metropolitan Housing Trust: a welcome additional 32 homes in all. But the biggest innovation during this time was the Trust expanding its provision of care and support services, and extending it well beyond its own tenants.

Expanding care and support
The Trust set up **Hornsey Care and Support** as a subsidiary in 2004, to make good use of the new provisions of the government's *Supporting People* programme, introduced nationally in 2003. There had previously been a range of separate funding streams financing additional support for vulnerable people to enable them to live independently: support which went beyond help with their care or day-to-day living costs. Supporting People pooled all the funding streams, including some elements of service charges previously eligible for Housing Benefit, and allocated a block grant to each local authority to spend as it determined. In each local authority area, there would already have been a multiplicity of support schemes for different groups (for example, ex-prisoners, people fleeing domestic violence, recovering drug and alcohol users) as well as older people

Street property at Rathcoole Gardens N8

needing support. While existing services, such as Hornsey Housing Trust's sheltered housing schemes, would have had high priority for continued funding, there was scope for services to expand, given council support. Indeed, the estimate of a later research paper was that the Supporting People budget almost doubled the previous expenditure on support of this type (House of Commons Research Paper 12/40 16 July 2012).

Hornsey Care and Support flourished for six years, employing over 70 people at its peak, and focussing on help for vulnerable older people. It provided support for the Trust's own tenants, both permanently for those in sheltered housing, and also floating support for tenants in street properties when their needs required it. It went on to win a contract to provide similar support to 140 older and disabled people in the London Borough of Barnet, in partnership with Barnet's Social Services Department. It joined with the Novas Group to create the '*60+ in Haringey*' scheme, supporting a further 300 older people across the borough, from all tenure groups. And working with the local Primary Care Trust, it provided short-term care to support patients recently discharged from hospital. The Annual Reports of the organisation, held by the Financial Conduct Authority, show that by 2007/08 Hornsey Care and Support had a turnover of £1.6M, and significant reserves.

The project finally foundered, as did so many others, with the financial cutbacks following the world-wide banking crisis of 2008. In 2009, the 'ring fence' that had prevented Supporting People grant being used for other programmes was removed by government. Local authorities everywhere, experiencing cuts in their central grants, were faced with invidious choices about which services they could continue to fund. For Hornsey Care and Support, turnover was down to £88K in 2009/10, and registered as nil in 2010/11.

Relationships

Tenants continued to be involved in many aspects of the Trust's activities, including membership of the Committee of Management, now called the Board. By 2005 there was a fully fledged **Tenants' Federation** at the Trust:

> *'Membership comprises fourteen tenant representatives who stand for election by all of the Trust's tenants. (It) meets at least quarterly and elects three representatives to sit on the Board. The Tenants' Federation also nominates members to take part in best value services review panels, the production of tenant newsletters and meetings with contractors and external organisations.* (Annual Report, 2004/05)

The Trust continued the innovative and unusual practice of inviting all tenants to the Annual General Meeting of the Trust until the 2012 AGM, about which more later. It seems to have been a significant annual event in the social calendar.

During the first decade of this period, the Trust continued to maintain a close working relationship with **Haringey Council**. There was frequent contact with the Housing team over nominating tenants for the newly built homes, and also to the vacancies which arose from time to time. The Council set up a Housing Forum for social housing

Christmas party at the Moravian Church Hall, Hornsey

providers in the Borough – including its own council housing, now run by an Arms Length Management Organisation – which Andrew Billany chaired. Relations with the Social Services team, previously focussed on the needs of individual tenants, now developed much more fully through the administration of the Supporting People grant to Hornsey Care and Support.

The Trust won competitive funding from the **Department of Health** to make further adaptations to Abyssinia Court to help it to develop into an 'extra care' scheme if needed. This was prompted in part by a Trust tenant, whose partner needed extra support, who expressed the wish that they both be helped to remain together in their home. Meanwhile, the Trust continued to play an active role in the **Solomon Project**, initiated in 1999 by several small housing associations working in North London, to pool and share expertise, insights and potentially services.

Rent setting

A significant change to national housing policy was made in these early years of the new century, which would impact the Trust along with all other social landlords. This was the introduction of rent setting by a nationally agreed formula in 2001. From its inception until 1972, the Trust had set its own rents (other than in periods of rent freeze, such as wartime). From 1972 till 1989, 'fair rents' negotiated between landlord and tenant and approved by the local rent officer had been the law (and are still in place for the handful of Trust tenants who took up their tenancies before the later date). From 1989, housing associations were again able – like councils – to set their own rents. Inevitably, rents in local areas began to diverge, as each social landlord developed their own policy on rent-setting and rent increases, tailored to their own financial situation. The government green paper 'Quality and Choice' (2000) identified this divergence as a problem, and rehearsed a range of solutions with the aim *'that social housing rents on similar houses in the same area should be the same, no matter who is the landlord'*.

The eventual outcome was the introduction of a 'formula rent' in 2002 which took into account both local capital values (reflecting size, desirability etc) and regional earnings (reflecting affordability); and annually uprated. This was the rent that would be set for any new letting, while existing tenants would move towards it in prescribed steps. It is surprising, with hindsight, how little objection was made at the time by social landlords – particularly local authorities – who were to lose the power to set their own rents. One compensation, for the first few years at least, was that the annual upratings were set at slightly above the level of inflation. For government, liable to pay rent rebates and rent allowances (the forerunners of Housing Benefit) it was a huge advantage to finally be in control of the levels of rent which social landlords charged. It did not become apparent till the next decade how sweepingly government might exercise that control in a time of austerity, to restrict its welfare spending.

Unsettled years
The middle years of these two decades were unsettled for the Trust, evidenced by a succession of at least five interim Chief Executives after Andrew Billany's departure, between 2008 and 2012, and changes in the membership of the Board and its chairs. A key question which underlay this period was whether the Trust was too small to be capable of remaining an independent body and should instead merge its activities with another housing association. This issue is cited by some as a contributory *cause* of the disturbance – a reason for so many interim CEO appointments; but by others as a *response* to the disruption – a way of sorting things out. The Trust was one of many small housing associations considering this option at this time, in the wake of the global financial upset of 2008, and facing a national 'austerity' strategy.

The disadvantages of staying small and independent are partly financial. A small housing association does not have the reserves and financial robustness of a larger organisation, and may be more vulnerable to financial shocks. But there are other factors too: functions which in a larger organisation are performed in-house – legal, finance, development – have to be brought in from outside, and may not be as closely attuned to the organisation's values and circumstances. A significant issue for a small housing association is its day-to-day repair and maintenance service; it may be too big to rely on local tradespeople, but too small to get a responsive service from the larger regional builders. And then a small staff team means fewer opportunities for promotion, so an officer who wants to progress in their career may have to move elsewhere.

On the other hand, despite these practical disadvantages, staying small has some advantages. A small association may be able to maintain better connections with its local community, for the benefit of its tenants and their neighbours, including using – as the Trust does – a variety of nearby community halls, schools and churches for events. Staff may know their tenants better, and have a clearer understanding of the services that they need and value; and in a small staff team, a higher proportion will be working on the front line, able to have their voices heard within the organisation. Tenants may be more likely to know and look out for each other, and report any concerns about their neighbours. When things go wrong (and something always will) there is a local office where tenants can go to say so, and there are local councillors to complain to who will be able to get a response from the association. And the Board may be a real resource: a strong Board, made up of people with a variety of skills and experience – often living locally themselves – can offer a lot of time and support to a small association, and exert a significant influence on it. Of course, not all small housing associations offer these advantages; but they can work towards them, and both tenants and Board members can help in that enterprise. Whereas if – because of the organisational difficulties set out above – they merge with a larger association, there is no guarantee that tenants will receive a better or more responsive service from their landlord; and there may be less scope to get things put right when they go wrong.

We do not have the Board minutes from this period to trace how the debate progressed, and these arguments were weighed up, but we do know that in 2011, the decision was taken to remain independent. However, the issue had proved divisive, and relations between some Board members, staff and tenants remained difficult. Matters came to a head at a chaotic AGM in 2012, to which (as was still the practice) all tenants had been invited, with proceedings which warranted an article in the specialist housing press. At around the same time, serious concerns about the governance of the Trust led to the involvement of the Homes and Communities Agency (HCA), the government regulator of social housing. The Trust was asked to undertake a review of its governance, and enter into a Voluntary Undertaking, an opportunity to put things right before more formal intervention by the HCA. Late in 2012 a new Chair (Greg Gordon) was elected; an adviser, widely respected in the housing world, was appointed to help the Trust through this period; and Pinnacle Housing Group, a professional housing management organisation working with councils and housing associations, was brought in to assist. Within the year, there was an almost entirely new Board, and an almost entirely new staff team.

Settling down and taking stock

In December 2013, with a permanent CEO due to be appointed, the Trust published a detailed Business Plan with ambitious aspirations. Many of these related to improving day-to-day housing management, for instance reducing the time it took to relet properties and improving rent collection. A central concern was the state of the Trust's older housing, and the strategy here was to develop a property maintenance plan underpinned by a detailed stock condition survey, to ensure that homes were fit for purpose. New building was also planned, dependant on funding. The appointment of Alwyn Lewis who had led the Pinnacle team, as the new permanent Chief Executive, helped establish stability and continuity. One early decision was not to maintain an independent waiting list, but to offer Haringey Council the right to nominate new tenants to vacant flats.

The Annual Reports of the next few years provide further evidence of an organisation settling down after a difficult time. '*After a number of years of under-investment in our properties*' (AR 2012/13), a programme of works commenced which would upgrade both the physical structure of many Trust properties (new windows, kitchens and bathrooms) and also installations such as boilers and door entry systems, with lifecycle assessments of the various components of a dwelling. One initiative was the mounting of solar panels on the roof of Margaret Hill House. In parallel with the stock condition survey, the Trust carried out a full tenancy audit. This brought to light some concerns which needed managing – examples of hoarding,

Solar panels at Margaret Hill House

for instance, and furniture and decorations in the common areas of shared houses which would present a risk in case of evacuation due to fire; it also identified the need for greater support for some tenants. A few instances of unlawful subletting were also found.

As well as investment to maintain and improve its existing older housing, the Trust started to consider how to achieve its ambitions for new development. Reviewing its existing properties, space for additional flats was identified at Abyssinia Court, Palm Tree Court, and Norah Clegg House, 21 flats in all, and architects began the process of drawing up schemes and securing the necessary planning permissions. Meanwhile, attention was also being paid to the relationship – formal and informal – between the Trust and its tenants.

Tenant engagement

The 'unsettled years' clearly disrupted the formal relationship between the Trust and its tenants in the early years of this final decade. The Trust took the decision in 2013 no longer to include tenants on the Board but instead to set up a **Tenant Scrutiny Panel** as an alternative, and early on engaged a representative from the Tenant Participation Advisory Service to chair it. Not surprisingly, some of the tenants interested in participation were not supportive of these decisions. For a while the Panel worked effectively, meeting after each Board meeting to review decisions taken, assisting in the selection of a new repairs organisation, in monitoring the contract, and in post-inspection of voids. But over time it worked less well, and was eventually wound up, although individual tenants continued to be involved in significant issues affecting the Trust.

However, during this period informal tenant engagement began to flourish, especially at the sheltered schemes where managers organised regular get-togethers, a Stroke club, exercise classes and outings. A Christmas party and a summer Barbeque, open to all tenants, became fixtures in the calendar. A local organisation, Active Age Crouch End, established a popular weekly get-together at Margaret Hill House for its tenants and older members of the local community; and also ran a monthly lunch open to all tenants and staff at Abyssinia Court. A regular newsletter for tenants – The Link – was established, and a Tenant Engagement Strategy was drafted, and redrafted. Discussions were held with Homes for Haringey (which managed the Council's housing stock) about developing a policy of sheltered housing 'hubs' where a range of activities would be located open to older people living in that neighbourhood.

The development of a good relationship with the **Alzheimer's Society**, led to the establishment of a weekly 'Dementia Café' at Abyssinia Court, with a range of participatory activities for tenants and neighbours, and their families and friends. Building on this, the Trust became a key player in Haringey's Dementia Action Alliance, chaired by Alwyn Lewis, which included over 30 local organisations committed to improving life in the borough for those with dementia and their families.

An initiative by one scheme manager led to the publication by Hornsey Historical Society and Hornsey Housing Trust of **'Memories of Tenants of Margaret Hill House'**, which traced the life stories of several residents and the varied journeys they had taken to becoming tenants of Hornsey Housing Trust: the book was launched in Crouch End with Catherine West, MP for Hornsey & Wood Green. In 2016/17 LB Haringey's independent assessment recorded a 90% satisfaction rating from tenants of the Trust's sheltered schemes.

L-R: Hephzibah Lewis, Phil Dart and Catherine West MP at the launch of the 'Memories of Tenants of Margaret Hill House' book ©Nick Edwards

Income and expenditure

Following the 2015 General Election, a change to the government's rent policy presented an immediate challenge to the Trust's ability to match its expenditure with its income. For the four years 2016 – 2020, instead of the usual permitted annual rent increase of inflation-plus-0.5/1%, with which social housing landlords had become familiar, the government prescribed an actual rent reduction of 1% pa. This measure was forecast to save £1.4 billion of government spending on Housing Benefit, at a time when the 'austerity' policy was in full swing. One justification cited at the time was that some social landlords had built up significant surpluses over the years, as they paid off loans taken out at the time their housing stock was built. But for a small housing association like Hornsey Housing Trust, without substantial surpluses and with recent new building which still had to be paid for, balancing the books became a more difficult task.

One option the Board rejected was that of charging a higher rent (called 'affordable', up to 80% of market value) on reletting properties when they became vacant. This might have generated marginally more income, but with vacancies arising randomly throughout the stock, it ran the risk of creating a major problem of perceived unfairness between neighbours. In the event, through a scrupulous review of its service charges, and its day to day expenditure, the Trust managed to cope. Responding to the roll-out of Universal Credit in Haringey, one interesting initiative was to appoint a part time officer to help tenants with housing benefit advice, applications and appeals. In his first year he dealt with 120 cases, resulting in £26,000 of successful claims, to the benefit of both the tenants concerned, and the Trust.

The question of independence

Central to this most recent decade of the Trust's 90 years have been the issues identified above: maintaining its properties; tenant

Thursday October 8, 2015, H&H Series 7

NEWS

Trust rejects Right to Buy involvement

Hornsey Housing Trust has voted against voluntary participation in the extension of the Right to Buy scheme to housing association properties.

As a result of the government's scheme, replacement housing would be funded using receipts from councils selling off their own most valuable properties.

"We support the tenant's right to home ownership, but this should not result in the sale of council housing to subsidise any discounts," said Greg Gordon, Chair of Hornsey Housing Trust.

"As a small Housing Association, and with the high costs of land in the west of the borough, the Trust is concerned that we will not be able to replace any homes that are sold."

The vote, which was found overall in favour, was staged by the National Housing Federation.

A Haringey Council spokeswoman said: "We've joined other councils in calling on the government to review both their draconian restrictions on how Right to But receipts can be reinvested and their proposals to extend the policy to housing association tenants, a move that would further choke the supply of new homes in London."

A further issue which faced the Board related to the 'Right to Buy'. Since this policy was introduced for Council tenants in 1980, giving them the right to purchase their rented Council property at a discounted price, attempts had been made to extend the policy to housing association tenants. A key problem was that housing associations were independent bodies, many of them charities, and it was difficult to see how they could be forced to sell assets, especially at less than their value. One option presented to housing associations in 2015 was to adopt the policy voluntarily. As can be seen from this news report the Board rejected this option, on both pragmatic and principled grounds.

Image reproduced by kind permission of the Hampstead & Highgate Express

engagement; balancing the books; and new development. For a while, though, in the middle of the decade, the dominant issue was once more the Trust's continued existence as an independent organisation. This question, which had threaded its way through Board discussions since the 'unsettled years', took solid shape again in 2016 and 2017. Aided by a consultancy, the Trust undertook an extensive Options Appraisal, reviewing whether to remain independent; to seek to work in partnership with other housing associations (sharing services, for example); or to pursue a full merger. Discussions were undertaken with several possible 'partners'; but in the event – as a few years before – the Board decided in 2017 that it preferred to *'maximise the advantages of independence and minimise the disadvantages'*, remaining small and independent, while open to joint working. These considerations were not unique to this Trust at that time: the external pressures of 'austerity' caused many small housing associations to review their financial stability, and led to the National Housing Federation publishing guidance on mergers in 2015. However, in choosing independence, the Trust was not alone. The large majority of housing associations remain relatively small: over 80% of registered providers in England manage fewer than 1,000 homes each (Regulator of Social Housing, 2022).

New homes for old
From late 2017, a major focus of the Trust became its programme to develop new homes in its existing developments (funded through capital, not revenue, expenditure). The start of building work early in 2018 meant significant disruption for the tenants already living on all three of the sites, as well as for staff based in the main Trust offices at Abyssinia Court. And the development programme itself was not without problems. These were partly a function of the complexity of the work, which in the case of Abyssinia Court and Palm Tree Court entailed fitting new flats within, or next to, already complicated buildings. It was also the case, however, that embarking on development again after a period of years entailed a steep learning curve for the Trust, and at one point required the employment of a specialist adviser to protect its interests and restrict cost and time overruns. But whatever the difficulties with the process – and there were many – there was no doubting the quality of the flats that were built, a perception reinforced by a recent survey of the tenants living there which showed a high degree of satisfaction with them.

Haringey Council had supported the building costs with grant aid from their Right to Buy receipts. The rest of the funding came partly

Top left: Extension to sheltered housing at Palm Tree Court, built 2019 ©HHT

Top right: New homes at Oakfield Road 2019 © HHT

Middle: Architects' drawing of Palm Tree Court including new flats on right ©HHT

Right: One of the new flats at Abyssinia Court, 2019

from the Trust's reserves, and partly from the proceeds of the sale of two properties in Hatherley Gardens. These sales were undertaken in part to fulfil a different policy, the houses including as they did eight bedsits. At the time the Trust owned 29 bedsits, distributed among twelve street properties. The problem they presented was that they were hard to let, partly because of the limitations of living in one room, but also because many – 11 – were located on the second floor with no lift access, and older people were reluctant to take them on knowing that they might find the stairs difficult in the future. (Indeed this was thought to be one reason why the Trust changed the age limit for lettings from 55 to 45 at the turn of the century, to widen the pool of prospective tenants). Reconfiguration was possible with some houses, but not many. The sale of two unpopular properties to help build more popular, modern, accessible flats therefore solved two problems at once.

    The larger issue this raises, though, is one which social housing landlords often find difficult to address. It is the Trust's settled policy (reflected in a number of Annual Reports) that some existing street properties could be sold to finance the construction of new flats purpose-designed for older people. The theory is fine: some converted flats are poorly designed or hard to access, and not well suited to the needs of older people, living as we must with the frailties that progress with our age. The developing concerns about climate change are another good reason to consider the advantages of well-designed new buildings, side by side with retrofitting existing dwellings. Older tenants who spend much of each day indoors, and may be living on a fixed income, need homes which can be warmed economically in winter and kept cool in summer, and in some cases that will be best achieved with a purpose built property.

    But in practice, for tenants of older properties, who may have called their flat 'home' for a long time, the prospect of moving may seem daunting. This issue arose at Goldsmiths' Court during this period, when discussions were held over some years with Haringey Council about the redevelopment of the corner of Shepherds Hill and Archway Road, incorporating this now ageing block of flats. While the project did not materialise, many tenants of Goldsmiths' Court found the prospect unsettling, not least because of the protracted period of uncertainty. This has been recognised by the Trust, which is now involved in collaborative discussion with tenants about improving standards of accommodation at Goldsmiths.

The COVID pandemic
Hot on the heels of the strains that the enforced rent reduction and the new homes development programme placed on the organisation, came COVID. It is hard to overstate the effect that the advent of the pandemic in early 2020 had on the Trust and its tenants – as on all of us. For a number of months staff largely worked from home, contacting tenants by phone – daily for those living in sheltered schemes, weekly for those living in street properties. Inevitably, all of the social engagement activities were put on hold, amid concerns about the increased isolation that some would experience. Adaptations had to be made to how the repairs service worked, with both tenants and operatives reluctant to come into contact. Staff, local voluntary groups and Haringey Council set up arrangements for support with shopping and prescriptions. Meetings of the leadership team, staff, and the Board took place virtually. And the usual Christmas party was replaced in December 2020 with the delivery of a hot meal to the 60 tenants who requested it. Tenants and staff have all welcomed being able to mingle and mix again.

The first ninety years
Many things have changed since Margaret Hill set up Hornsey Housing Trust ninety years ago. In 1933, two-thirds of households in England rented in the private sector, and only a fifth were owner-occupiers.

A tree was planted in Priory Park, Crouch End in April 2023 to celebrate the 90th anniversary. L-R: Euan Barr (HHT), Harifat Dada (Margaret Hill House tenant), Ian Roberts (HHT Board member), Eileen Kirkham (Margaret Hill House tenant), Barbara Moore (HHT), Cllr Dana Carlin, Catherine West MP, Cllr Adam Jogee, Joanne McCartney AM. ©David X Green

Councils had started to provide housing, encouraged by Government subsidies, but their main responsibilities were to rehouse those they were displacing through slum clearance. In Hornsey, there were many overcrowded households paying high rents, but the houses themselves were generally sound, and of a good size. Hornsey Housing Trust's innovation was to use local houses to meet local housing needs, and to use finance raised locally (from private investors and Hornsey Borough Council) to do so. It was not competing with the Council, which had a different job to do; but it was – like the Council – providing decent housing at a reasonable rent to local residents. This role, both complementing and supplementing council housing, was one which other housing associations adopted.

The urge to build a new Britain after the second world war led to a political consensus that local authorities should be encouraged to provide new housing, and that higher standards of housing quality should be enforced in both the public and the private sectors. By the 1970s, close to a third of all households lived in council and housing association housing, and over half were owner-occupiers, while the private rented sector was in what seemed like terminal decline. And as housing tenure has changed, housing conditions have improved enormously. Few households today would contemplate living without access to a fridge, or a cooker, or the use of a bath. And for most, renting a room in a shared house is for the young, at a particular stage in their lives, before they 'settle down'.

Hornsey Housing Trust responded to these changes, in the latter part of the twentieth century, by improving and self-containing its own homes; by developing supported housing to meet its own tenants' needs as they became older; and by seeking out other needs to meet within the borough, in particular those of different cultural and ethnic groups. What of the future? Three pieces of evidence suggest that the demand for what the Trust has to offer will only increase. First, more of us are living to an older age: life expectancy is much greater than ninety years ago. Secondly, because we are living longer, we are living with health and mobility conditions which may mean we need more suitable housing. And finally, more of us will be growing old in the private rented sector, with its insecurity and lack of rent control: since the millennium the private rented sector has more than doubled in size as the social housing and owner-occupied sectors have shrunk. There will be a lot of work for the Trust still to do.

Hornsey Housing Trust today, and looking ahead

Euan Barr, Chief Executive

What does Hornsey Housing Trust look like today and what are its plans for the future? The table overleaf provides a snapshot of the Trust in 2023 and its tenants, homes, Board and staff. As the year closes, the Board is considering its vision and Corporate Plan for the coming five years. This chapter picks out the key aspects the Trust is thinking about as it looks to the future.

Financial security

The challenges of surviving as a small housing association are discussed in earlier chapters, and with the increased regulation of recent years, they are becoming more acute for an organisation which charges low rents and is subject to government control of its rent setting. Balancing the books will continue to be the primary aim of the Trust as it seeks to remain independent. The Trust has secured some loan funding to help pay for improvement and growth and will pursue more grant funding opportunities. At the same time, it aims to ensure that it delivers cost efficiencies in the procurement of services, homes which are uncomplicated to maintain, robust management of its income and a close analysis of the risks it faces.

Tenant participation

In 2022 the Tenant Engagement Strategy was refreshed, and the Board and incoming Chief Executive in 2023 have increased efforts to involve tenants in all areas of activity, including in the recent recruitment of board members and staff, service area reviews, consultant appointments, setting design standards, and improving how the Trust communicates with its tenants. A new Tenant Panel has been set up, taking time to ensure that it defines its terms of

Hornsey Housing Trust 2023

Our homes
- 137 sheltered housing flats in seven schemes
- 232 homes in 59 street properties and small blocks of flats
- All in London Borough of Haringey, most in Hornsey N8

Our staff
We employ 13 staff:
- Six in housing management, tenancy and support roles
- Five in finance and back-office support
- One asset (property maintenance) manager
- Chief Executive

Our board
- We have nine voluntary, unpaid board members
- Two are current or former housing association chief executives
- Four are or were employed by medium to large housing associations
- Three have housing finance expertise
- Three are current local authority employees
- Other skills include housing asset management, development & regeneration, research and human resources

Our tenants
- 90% live alone
- 85% have their income supplemented by housing benefit or universal credit
- The average age of our sheltered/supported tenants is 75, for street property tenants it is 65
- 28% have been our tenants for over 15 years, 44% for over ten years
- 8–10% of our flats are re-let each year, mostly nominated by LB Haringey

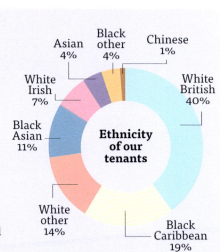

Ethnicity of our tenants: White British 40%, Black Caribbean 19%, White other 14%, Black Asian 11%, White Irish 7%, Asian 4%, Black other 4%, Chinese 1%

reference, its purpose, and its interaction and influence with the Board. While formal meeting structures are important, having a flexible and everyday approach to tenant involvement is proving equally beneficial.

All of this is consistent with regulatory aims to amplify 'tenant voice'. It is also a recognition that the Trust's tenants have a range of skills and life experience to offer and that it is particularly practical for a small, community-based organisation to seek the perspective of tenants in decisions made about the services they receive.

As the health and wellbeing benefits of remaining active and involved in older age are increasingly promoted, some tenants have expressed recent interest in volunteering. The Trust is currently establishing a framework for this to emphasise the interests of tenants, to promote service improvement and to ensure people have appropriate training. We have limited staff resources, and delivery of the aforementioned 'hub' concept (promoted widely within the 2022 'Better Social Housing Review' of the NHF/CIH) may well rely on effective volunteering to make it an enduring success.

Looking after properties day to day
The Trust has endured difficulties with its repairs service over the past decade, and associated dissatisfaction from residents and disillusionment amongst staff. The Board took the decision in 2023 to consider departure from the convention to outsource to big contractors. In some ways inspired by the early days of the Trust, it is looking at the possibility of doing more of its repair work 'in house', by operatives directly employed by the Trust: people who will develop familiarity with the stock, good relations with tenants and hopefully a more responsive service which makes everyone a lot happier. There is much to work through in terms of risks, planning and mobilisation, but it's an exciting prospect.

Property improvement & decarbonisation

Throughout the 90 year life of Hornsey Housing Trust, there have been several cycles of planned maintenance and improvement, particularly within the street properties, many of which are now more than a century old. This is a normal process for any well-managed housing association, and typically includes kitchen and bathroom replacements, new windows and doors, decorations and more significant works like roof covering renewals.

The last few years have introduced new and costly dimensions to managing property assets. Building safety (informed by the Building Safety Act 2022 and Social Housing Act 2023) and decarbonisation (Clean Growth Strategy 2017 and COP26 Climate Change Conference in Glasgow 2021) are areas where the Trust is expected to extend its conventional planned maintenance activity to cover increasing property safety demands and to meet energy efficiency targets. There is also a pending update of the Decent Homes Standard, first introduced in 2000.

With low rents and limited annual surpluses, finding the money to meet these standards is a big challenge for the Trust. There are government funding initiatives, such as the Social Housing Decarbonisation Fund, improved prospect of grant funding for regeneration (as opposed to simply funding more homes); in addition, the relatively high value location of its properties means that sale of assets may generate funds to reinvest in such improvements. This is to be balanced against the competing priority to build new homes where old ones are lost, in order to avoid organisational shrinkage and further erosion of important rent revenue. The Trust has started to form its new Corporate Strategy for the period 2024–2029, to include financial projections which will consider all of these aspects as the Trust works to retain its independence into its centenary.

HHT Board members, September 2023 (L-R): Linmora Blair, Anne Waterhouse, Jessica Bembirgde, June Barnes (Chair), Matthew Bolwell, Ian Roberts, Stephen Ross. Not pictured: Dawn Matthews, Bekah Ryder

New homes

In 2023, Haringey Council has the 3rd highest rate of people in London Boroughs living in temporary accommodation. This is evident on review of the list of Council nominations received whenever the Trust has an empty property to relet.

Although the Trust's housing stock hasn't grown much in number in 20 years (385 homes in 2003, 391 today), the new development of the past decade has improved quality and accessibility across the estate. In 2023, the Trust worked with a group of tenants, some with lived experience of recently developed homes and others with technical design skills and interests, to produce a new development brief alongside Trust Board members and Archio, an architectural consultancy. The purpose of this exercise is to communicate design standards for new homes to professionals and developers, helping the Trust to more effectively meet the needs of its future tenants whilst considering both financial and climate costs in use.

Almost half of the Trust's homes today are located within the early 20th century buildings typical of the local street vernacular. Across the portfolio there are still bedsits, basement and attic flats accessed via several flights of stairs, in some cases with more stairs inside the flat itself. The 'new homes for old' approach described in the previous chapter remains an important part of the Trust's development vision, in particular where homes are identified as less desirable for tenants due to their size, condition and access difficulties, or have more expensive upkeep liabilities.

The Trust Board of today is, however, also mindful of the popularity of much of the traditional stock within its heartland and its important contribution to a mixed community where older people

HHT Staff members, September 2023 (L-R): Top: Euan Barr, Derek Gill, Phil Johnson. Second row: Indje Shahin, Casey Masters. Bottom row: Barbara Moore, Veronica Lindsay, Liz Hanley, Vishwanne Jagdeo, Maria Reyes, Mussa Djalo. Not pictured: Christopher Adegoroye; Samson Sunmonu

of fixed means can afford to live, close to the amenities and bustle of Hornsey, Crouch End and Tottenham. A fresh scoping exercise has been undertaken in 2023 to see where the Trust might make more of its current land and property assets, by remodeling or building additional homes where space will allow.

Partnership working

This history has shown how from its founding, the Trust has worked closely with its local council, first Hornsey Borough Council and now the London Borough of Haringey. From Margaret Hill onwards, many councillors have served on the Trust's Board; and the Council has provided welcome financial support for the Trust both from its own resources and as a channel for government funding. Both organisations continue to be in contact day-to-day on a host of issues: tenancy support, housing benefit queries, nominations to vacant flats, planning, and housing standards. This close working relationship has been a key driver of improving housing conditions in the borough for local residents.

Earlier chapters have described the ways in which, particularly in the last 20 years, the Trust has sought to work alongside others too on important issues of the day affecting its tenants. This includes its central role in the former Haringey Social Housing Forum and Solomon Project and more recently in chairing the Haringey Dementia Action Alliance. In 2022, a tenancy sustainment project was established with 3 other small housing associations, providing a vital welfare advice service in the face of a national cost of living crisis.

The Trust is continuing its commitment to partnerships in 2023 and beyond. It remains a member of the North River Alliance, primarily a development vehicle for small housing associations which is also now working on joint projects for decarbonisation work. This partnership will deliver grant funding from the GLA to facilitate the building of new homes across Haringey and support the Trust's development strategy

Tenants at the Trust's annual summer event, July 2023

ambitions. The recently increased emphasis on supply of social rented housing (as opposed to higher rates of 'affordable' housing rents) is consistent with the Trust's enduring commitment to this type of tenure.

It is also looking close to home, renewing its links with Hill Homes (referred to from the 'War Years' chapter onwards), a small Highgate-based housing and care organisation with a shared history, similar tenant demographic, community focus and many of the same operational challenges faced by the Trust. In 2023, we are in discussion about mutually accessing local tenant activities and hope to extend our talks into other areas of work.

A healthy & diverse community
In a wider sense, we are in discussion with The Centre for Ageing Better, which is pioneering ways to make ageing better a reality for everyone. This includes creating a network of 'Age-friendly Communities' which are places committed to ageing well and living a good later life. Its vision is for people to stay living in their homes, participate in the activities they value, and contribute to their communities, for as long as possible – important parallels with the aims

of the Trust. As Haringey doesn't presently have this status, we have opened discussions with the Council and other local organisations to promote it. The Haringey 'State of the Borough' report published in April 2023 projects that the over 65 population will increase by 40%, from 27,700 to 40,000, by 2030. Overall, the west of the Borough is expected to see the highest increases in older population.

There is a sharper increase predicted in people over 85 from ethnic minority backgrounds. Earlier chapters have discussed the expansion phase of the 1980s and 90s, where the Trust took a progressive approach to house a mix of ethnic groups to provide peer support and create mixed communities. The expected increasing need of an older population from a wider range of people from ethnic minority backgrounds, presents an opportunity for the Trust to lead a person-centred approach to independent living, as well as connecting people to the support they need to manage the health challenges of living longer and using our sheltered hubs for a range of activities. The Trust's tenant population broadly reflects the ethnic diversity of Haringey. The Trust Board of 2023 – itself ethnically diverse – aims to ensure that tenant involvement is similarly representative (in both geography and protected characteristics) to bring a broad range of perspectives to the development of its services.

For a number of decades now, Hornsey Housing Trust's motto has been 'More Than Just Housing', a phrase which reflects the ideals of its founder, Margaret Hill, who was concerned above all with how to live well as we age. Margaret Hill would herself recognise many of the addresses amongst the Trust's homes still. And we are sure she would be pleased that the Trust is still doing the job she set it up to do: providing people with a place to call home.

Acknowledgements

This history could not have been written without the contributions of many people who have been involved in the work of Hornsey Housing Trust over the years, including current and previous staff, Board members and tenants. Amongst them are June Barnes, Euan Barr, Andrew Billany, Andy Fletcher, Shirley Graham, Julie-Ann Gregory, David Hargreaves, Michele and Haroun Jogee, Phil Johnson, Alwyn Lewis, Steve Lord, and Olexandra Stepaniuk, and I'd like to thank them all. It was particularly helpful to be lent a copy of the unpublished biography of Margaret Hill, and I'm grateful to her grandchildren Nicholas and Charlotte Humphrey and the author Carole Angier for their support. I'd also like to acknowledge the help of the volunteers of the Hornsey Historical Society and the staff of Bruce Castle Museum and the London Metropolitan Archives. Any errors of fact or interpretation are mine.

Rosie Boughton

Bibliography and Archives

Angier, Carole	**Margaret Hill** (completed 1979, not published)
Denford, Steven	**Hornsey Past** (Historical Publications, 2008)
Gay, Ken	**From Forest to Suburb** (HHS 1988)
Gay, Ken	**Hornsey and Crouch End** (The History Press, 1998)
Hill, Margaret	**An Approach to Old Age and its Problems** (Oliver and Boyd, 1961)
Holtby, Winifred	**South Riding** (Collins, 1936)
Kosky, Jules	**The Top of the Hill, a history of Hill Homes** (Hill Homes, 1994)
Orwell, George	**The Road to Wigan Pier** (Gollancz 1937, Penguin 1962)
Shute, Nevil	**Ruined City** (Cassell, 1938, Pan 1963)
Smith, Mary	**Guide to Housing** (SHAC 1977, 2nd ed)
Whitehead, Jack	**The Growth of Muswell Hill** (Jack Whitehead, 1995)

Memories of tenants of Margaret Hill House (HHT/HHS 2017)
Hornsey Housing Trust Archives and London Metropolitan Archives (see overleaf)

Hornsey Housing Trust Archives

HHT Ref	Document	Date
AGM1	AGM Annual Report and Accounts	1933–1957
AGM2	AGM Minutes	1938–1999
AGM3	AGM signing in book	1997–2008
AGM4	Occasional additional annual reports	Various
CR1	Chairman's reports	1934–1957
RU1	Set of Rules/use of seal	1992
TA1	Tenants' Assistance Fund report book	1935–1940
TA2	Tenants' Assistance Fund report book	1940–1953
TA3	Tenants' Assistance Fund annual reports	1936, 1938
CM1	Committee of Management minutes	1949–1974
CM2	Committee of Management minutes	1974–1984
LS1	Request for loan stock	1933
LS2	Prospectus for loan stock	1938
LS3	Loan Stock Register	1938–1999
LS4	Letter of redemption of loan stock	2005
SH1	Share ledger	1954–1996
SH2	Share certificate records	1961–2012
SH3	Share Certificate book	1972–2012
SH4	Register of members and shares	1996–2012
SH5	Occasional list of members	1979–1990
PR1	Property register	1933–1991
PR2	Auction catalogue	1937
PR3	Property insurance schedules	1960s–90s
MS1	'An experiment in housing'	1934
MS2	File of press and other cuttings	1938–2003
MS3	Photo/slide library	1980s/1990s
MS4	Diamond Jubilee event	1993

AGM Annual General Meeting
RU Rules
CM Committee of Management/Board
SH Shares
MS Miscellaneous

CR Chairman's reports
TA Tenants' Assistance Fund
LS Loan Stock
PR Property records